PINOCCHIO'S QUEST

By
Robert Rogland

CHRISTIAN LIBERTY PRESS

Author: Robert Rogland
Editor: Michael J. McHugh
Copy Editor: Diane C. Olson
Artist: Vic Lockman
Image Colorization: Bob Fine
Cover Colorization: Christopher Kou
Design: Bob Fine

Ad maiorem Dei gloriam

Christian Liberty Press
502 W. Euclid Avenue
Arlington Heights, IL 60004
www.christianlibertypress.com

ISBN 978-1-932971-11-8

— Contents —

To my wife

— Preface —

The classic story of Pinocchio has delighted young people for over a century. During the twentieth century, several different versions of this time-honored story were published which contained a variety of plots and moral themes. Never before, however, has any author endeavored to complete a version of the Pinocchio story that is both morally uplifting and true to the message of the Gospel of Jesus Christ—that is, until the completion of *Pinocchio's Quest*!

As most readers realize, the Pinocchio story by its very nature contains a steady dose of imaginative fiction. The book that follows is no exception. The author, Robert Rogland, has endeavored to present real biblical truth through the use of an action-packed fantasy novel. It is the hope of the author and publisher that each reader will realize that although *Pinocchio's Quest* is fictional and beyond the limits of reality, it is also a work that contains vitally important spiritual symbolism and moral principles that are grounded in the eternal truths of Holy Scripture. The story of Pinocchio that follows, therefore, is designed to not only entertain readers, but to challenge them on a spiritual level.

May God be pleased to use this unique novel to bless the lives of all who read its pages, and to help such ones to begin their own quest to find salvation in the person and work of Christ alone.

Michael J. McHugh
Arlington Heights, Illinois
2000

PINOCCHIO'S HOME
ROMAGNANO
VERCELLI
PO RIVER
CASALE
TORINO
ALESSANDRIA
NOVI
GENOA
PORTOFINO
DR. MORO'S ISLAND
ADRIATIC SEA
ITALY
LIGURIAN SEA
CORSICA
SARDINIA
TYRRHENIAN SEA
SICILY

Chapter 1

I am the boy who was once a log; I am the boy who traveled over land and sea seeking to be changed; I am the boy who was born again in a whale. Many have told my story, but not one of them got it right. I suppose I must tell it myself.

I first saw the light of day in a village so small it had no name. No stranger passing through its twisting streets would have suspected that the two greatest woodcarvers in Italy lived there, unless he turned aside from his business to browse in their shops.

The younger of these masters was my father, Gepetto. Nothing about Father's appearance suggested what an extraordinary man he was. Father was short, plump, and pear-shaped. He had a broad face with hazel eyes, a button nose, and a weak, clean-shaven chin. At the time of my creation Father was fifty years old. His hair, once chestnut brown and luxurious, had faded and shrunk to a grizzled fringe around a shiny dome. His skin still glowed a youthful pink, but lines now fanned out and up from the corners of his eyes and mouth, creating an impression of perpetual merriment.

Father looked like Saint Nicholas; and in our little village he played the part as well. He carved and painted wooden figures: dolls that brought sparkle to the eyes of even spoiled little rich girls; fierce dogs that put cats to flight, tails between their legs; gilded angels so glorious you knew the Lord himself was only a step behind. Father carved soldiers, hunchbacks, kings, crones—every character that delighted and amazed. And the animals! You would have sworn his butterflies, peacocks, and lobsters were real till you touched them. As for his lions and bears, … well, you would not have dared approach them to make the test.

Our other master carver was named Giuseppe. In appearance he was everything Father was not: tall and lanky, a mane of white hair cascading down to his shoulders, a white beard masking most of his face. Giuseppe was older than Father, but not a single line etched his pale face. His deep-set, coal-black eyes held your gaze whenever he spoke. In many respects, Giuseppe looked like a prophet.

Giuseppe's line was clocks—not ordinary cuckoo clocks like those turned out in every village and town between the great Po

River and the Alps, but one-of-a-kind creations that displayed the most cunning casework and intricate mechanisms to be found in the kingdom. Many of Giuseppe's timepieces were cuckoo clocks, of course, for some customers could imagine nothing else on their parlor wall. But buyers who wanted something unique always came away satisfied. Many of Giuseppe's most delightful clocks sported a little stage where wooden figures emerged from a door to perform amusing antics on the hour and half-hour. My own favorite featured a butcher waving a cleaver and pursuing a dog making off with his sausages.

Giuseppe fashioned his clocks entirely out of wood, except for the mainspring. None of his masterpieces ever broke down or wore out. Fifty years ago, Giuseppe carved his first clock to grace his own hearth. It hangs there still, keeping perfect time. Father appreciated Giuseppe's work as only another master craftsman can, and Giuseppe was Father's greatest admirer. For forty years, they were the best of friends.

Giuseppe was a happier man than Father, for he had a son, Giovanni, to carry on his name and work; but Father had never married. As a young man Father had found satisfaction and contentment enough in his craft, but as he grew older he began to long for a boy of his own. Thoughts of the son he did not have made Father more unhappy as the years passed. Once he felt pleasure watching a boy or girl leave his shop happily clutching a toy; now he would sigh as bright-eyed children ran home with their prizes, reminded once again that he had no son of his own to delight with his wonderful creations.

Father never spoke of his sorrow to anyone, but Giuseppe knew all the same and did his best to relieve Father's loneliness. Many nights the two men would get together for coffee and dominos. They would talk and laugh about old times, and Father would leave Giuseppe's house in high spirits at the end of the evening; but alone again at night in his empty house the sadness would return.

One spring day Father burst into Giuseppe's shop more excited than the older man had ever seen him before.

"Giuseppe, I just had a marvelous idea! What an inspiration! You can make me a happy man in my old age; you can make me a father!"

One spring day Father burst into Giuseppe's shop more excited than the older man had ever seen him before.

"Calm down, Friend. Sit here and take ten deep breaths before you speak—no, make it twenty. You know I would do whatever I could to bring you happiness, but making you a father is one thing I cannot do."

Gepetto rapidly inhaled and exhaled twenty times, then went on, just as breathless and beside himself as before.

"Really, Giuseppe, you can make me a father. I don't know why I didn't think of it before. I want my boy to have dark hair, and a nose just like mine, but lips not quite as thin. And freckles—he must have freckles."

Giuseppe cocked his head and squinted at Father. "I'm getting worried about you now, Gepetto. You're talking too fast to be joking and I know you're not drunk. I'm afraid you've become deranged. You must explain how I can make you a father or I'll have to call Doctor Luca."

"I'm sorry, Giuseppe. My tongue has run ahead of my thoughts; but I'm entirely sane, perfectly serious, and deliriously happy. You can make me a father, Giuseppe, only you. Listen, I'll explain."

"This is bound to be interesting. Proceed."

"I'll carve a wooden boy to be a son to me. I'll make him hollow. You'll fill him with gears and levers and whatnot to make him walk and talk and blink and cough and do all the things real boys do. You'll fit him out with a mainspring, and I'll wind him up when he needs it."

Stopping the torrent of words only to breathe, Father went on. "I know my boy will never grow up, but he'll be happier that way. He'll escape the sorrows that come with age, sorrows you and I know well enough. In fact, he'll escape death itself: After I'm gone someone else can wind him up. Well, what do you think?"

Giuseppe sat silently for a long time, his brow furrowed in thought. Father waited patiently, his face radiating a serene confidence that Giuseppe could and would do what he asked. When Giuseppe finally replied, he spoke slowly and gravely.

"Gepetto, I could do it. But do you know what you would be getting into? A wooden puppet that can walk and talk and do the things real boys do could bring you more sorrow than happiness. Children don't always make their parents proud; sometimes they bring them grief. Talk to the Martinis about their wayward Giovanni or the Respighis about their unfortunate Domenico.

They've had their troubles! You don't have the energy you had at twenty-five to discipline a woodenheaded son. Maybe you ought to think about this some more."

"No, I've been through all that in my mind. I want a boy of my own even if he turns out as lazy as Giovanni Martini or as stupid as Domenico Respighi. I will still love him. I want a boy of my own to *love*, Giuseppe. Do you understand?"

"I think so. In a way I too would be the boy's father, for we would share the joy of creating him. I would rejoice with you if he were a good boy; I would feel the same pain if he were bad. A part of me would be in him. Yes, I think I understand how you feel."

Giuseppe stopped talking and thought for a long time. Just as the silence was beginning to make Father uneasy, his friend stood up and grasped his hand.

"Very well. I agree to make you a father. You carve yourself a son just the way you want him on the outside and hollow him out. I'll take care of the works inside. We're in this together, for better or worse."

"Giuseppe, you've made me the happiest man in the village," responded Father.

"Old friend, let's hope so."

Chapter 2

Father wasted no time, but set to work as soon as he returned from Giuseppe's house. He selected a stock of well-seasoned cherry wood, a piece he had set aside in case he received a commission from a duke or bishop. He placed it on the bench and took down the box of charcoals from the shelf. Lovingly, reverently, Father began to sketch my features on the block of wood. He had no need for first drawings, for he saw me in his mind's eye as clearly as if I had been sitting on the bench under the lamp.

When he finished sketching, Father sharpened his chisels and knives until each could split the thinnest hair. Then he began to carve away the excess wood to expose the curly hair, noble nose (just like his own—Father had always been proud of his nose), full lips, and other features traced on the rich cherry wood.

It was well past midnight when Father laid down his tools to go to bed, but my head lay completed on the bench. If I say so myself, he had never carved a nobler face.

The next morning Father hollowed out my head and fashioned my tongue, jaw, and eyelids from other pieces of cherry. My teeth he made of white oak, for strength; my eyeballs he carved of beech wood, bleached even whiter, with ebony insets for the pupils. He did not attach the moving parts to the head, but left that to Giuseppe.

After he had finished carving my head and all its parts, Father made himself stop for a brief lunch and a coffee. Then he began working on my body. For my trunk he chose curly maple; for my arms and legs he selected straight-grained ash, strong and limber wood that would bend without breaking. Father had pictured me as a boy of average height and build, and such he made me. He worked through the afternoon and evening without stopping and finished my trunk and limbs by midnight of the second day.

The third day Father slept in. He was ready to paint me and did not rise till morning light was bright enough to show his paints in their true colors. Father brought me piece by piece into the paint room and hung my parts like laundry on cords strung from wall to wall. From a shelf piled high with tubes of colored pigments he selected white, burnt umber, vermilion, cobalt blue, rose madder, and black; then he prepared a palette with various flesh tones, auburn for my hair, and cornflower blue for my eyes.

Father was now ready to paint me in all the hues and tints of a real boy. Beginning with the crown of my head, he painted me down to the soles of my feet. If a customer had happened into the back room that afternoon, he would have had quite a shock. My head, arms, legs, and other body parts were hanging there drying, looking like so many joints of meat in the butcher's shop.

Father brought Giuseppe around to see his work.

"You have outdone yourself this time, Gepetto," pronounced Giuseppe after inspecting all my parts. "Anyone would think you were a fiend who dismembers little children foolish enough to wander into your den. Just look at the detail in that face! Freckles, a hint of sun, and dimples, too. And the eyes twinkle even before I've set them in their sockets. The girls are going to be broken-hearted when they discover that your boy feels nothing for them."

"Well, that's the way of the world, isn't it?" replied Father. "Besides," he added, "I'm hoping you can fix him up with a heart and smiles and tears. Walking and talking and blinking and coughing aren't enough, Giuseppe. Can't you make him feel and think, too? That professor who comes up every summer from Torino says men are just machines. Although I know men are not machines, you should be able to make my boy feel and think and act almost human. If anyone can do it, Giuseppe, you can."

Giuseppe didn't reply. The two friends remained silent as they wrapped my parts in paper and placed me in Giuseppe's wheelbarrow. Giuseppe spoke a final word to Father before he departed.

"I'll make your son as human as I can, with a heart and smiles and tears. But I may succeed too well. Such a son may break your heart and bring you more tears than smiles. Children sometimes do that, you know."

When Giuseppe arrived home, he unpacked my pieces and arranged them on his bench. He left me unassembled for several days as he busied himself at the drawing board designing the machinery that would give me life.

When he had completed all the drawings, Giuseppe tacked them to the wall above the bench and began to carve levers, gears, slides, racks, pinions, flywheels, and bearings. He gave me more moving parts than he had put in any of his previous creations. To drive the works he fitted me with a mainspring of fine Milano steel, which was wound by a key protruding from my back. Only the key revealed to the world that I was a machine; the rest of my works were greased and sealed inside the body Father made.

Giuseppe brought Father to his shop for the final assembly and winding.

"Are you ready, Gepetto? When I wind up your son, he will behave like a real boy, except that he will not be able to talk. I want you to have the joy of teaching your son to talk."

"May I wind him up, Giuseppe?"

"No," replied Giuseppe. "You'll do that every year for the rest of your life. I claim the privilege of winding him up the first time."

"How often should I wind him?"

"You should wind him up once a year to ensure that he has all the vigor a young boy needs. Your son probably could go thirteen months between windings, but he would be tired and listless the last month."

Giuseppe paused. He inserted the key into the keyhole in my back; it locked in place.

"Well, here we go."

With the first turn of the key I opened my eyes and became conscious of the light. With the second turn of the key I sat up and looked around. With the third turn of the key I stretched, yawned, and hopped down from the bench. Giuseppe picked me up, placed me back on the bench, and held me down firmly with his left hand while he turned the key nine more times with his right. I felt energetic and full of curiosity by the time he finished. I understood Giuseppe and Father perfectly as they spoke, but I myself could not yet speak.

Giuseppe took me by the hand and brought me to Father.

"Gepetto, here is your son. What are you going to name him?"

"I will call my son Pinocchio."

"Are you ready, Gepetto? When I wind up your son, he will behave like a real boy, except that he will not be able to talk.

Chapter 3

Laughing and crying, Father picked me up and kissed me, stroking my wooden curls and murmuring my name over and over. Then he began to dress me in the clothes he had brought: emerald knickers with yellow suspenders, a green and yellow checked shirt, lemon yellow knee stockings, sturdy black boots with brass buckles, and a green hat with a feather poking out at a rakish angle. Father liked yellow and green.

He tried to remove my key, but it was firmly locked in the middle of my back.

"Giuseppe, the key is stuck in the keyhole."

"I did that on purpose, Gepetto. A key that can be removed is a key that can be lost. Pinocchio's shirt will conceal it."

"You're right, of course. I can't be too careful with that key. It is truly the key of life for my wooden boy."

Father finished dressing me and let me explore Giuseppe's shop, which I was eager to do, while he embraced Giuseppe, thanking him a dozen times for giving him a son. Then he took me firmly by the hand and set off to show me to the neighbors.

The whole village knew what Father and Giuseppe were up to, for Father had explained the scheme to anyone who would listen. Few believed that even such masters as Gepetto and Giuseppe could make an active wooden boy; still, all eyes followed Father that morning as he hurried up the hill to Giuseppe's house. Surely Gepetto and Giuseppe had over-reached themselves this time. But no! Less than an hour later Father emerged from Giuseppe's shop with me in tow. The two men had done the impossible: they had made a wooden boy act like a real boy.

Every family was delighted when Father appeared at the door with a fidgeting wooden boy. We were whisked inside, the numerous children were gathered up and shushed, and Father was offered Italian soda or coffee to wet his whistle while he told the tale of my creation.

From aged grandparents to the youngest school children, the neighbors gaped shamelessly and poked me furtively when Father wasn't looking. Only the very young took no special notice of me.

In their eyes a wooden boy was no different from any other boy that walked and sat and drank milk, which I was given instead of wine or coffee.

Father never stopped talking the whole day. Before noon I heard the story of my creation told and retold in a half-dozen homes. Between houses Father told me the names of those we would visit next, who their relations were, what they did for a living, and how I should behave in their presence. I nodded to show that I understood, but did not try to talk. Indeed, I could not have gotten a word in if I had tried.

As the day wore on, wine and coffee loosened Father's tongue even more than the excitement of being a new father. By the time we arrived home he had told me of his father's experiences in the war, the history of Italy, the differences between Catholics and Waldenses (he was a Waldense), the merits of various kinds of pasta, and the travels of Marco Polo. In between these lectures he told me again and again how he loved me and hoped I would be happy, successful, and a credit to his name. We started home only when he lost his voice. The sun had already set.

For the first time, I entered my new home in one piece. Father lit the lamp.

"You must be hungry, Pinocchio," he rasped. "Tonight I have only bread and cheese for you. In the excitement of the last few days I forgot to shop. Tomorrow we'll go around to the shops and buy a proper supply of food for a growing boy."

He paused, then continued thoughtfully. "No, that's not right, is it? You'll never get bigger, though you will grow older and wiser. Oh, I have such high hopes for you, Pinocchio!"

Father would have gone on, but his voice gave out completely. He watched as I devoured the bread and cheese on my plate. Wordlessly he offered me more until I signaled, "Enough!" Then he showed me my bed. I had never seen a bed, but I knew at once what it was for and gladly climbed in, for wooden boys get tired as well as hungry. After he had tucked me in and kissed me, Father prayed soundlessly with moving lips. I had no idea what he was doing and was too tired to care.

As I lay in bed I tried to make sense of all I had seen and heard in my first day of life. Everything was etched perfectly in my memory, but I didn't grasp the meaning of what I had witnessed. Happiness, joy, excitement, and love were still strangers to me. It was too much to think about, and in a few minutes, I was asleep.

"No, that's not right, is it? You'll never get bigger, though you will grow older and wiser. Oh, I have such high hopes for you, Pinocchio!"

Chapter 4

In the weeks following my creation I learned to talk and behave altogether like a real boy.

My native village tumbled down the last worn foothill of the Alps and spilled out onto the wide plain of the Po. This nameless home of fewer than a thousand souls was a mass of light gray limestone houses roofed with dark orange terracotta tiles. Small as it was, our village was big enough to have a central square, or piazza, which lay on the valley floor at the very edge of the hill. The Catholic church, with a modest but lovely bell tower, anchored the east side of the piazza; the village hall, with an ornate tiled facade, bounded it on the west. Back from the square for several blocks in all directions, two story buildings overshadowed streets so narrow they saw sunlight only at noon. The piazza, of course, was bright all day long, and broiling hot in the summer. City people thought our village picturesque and quaint; and artists from Torino, Milano, Brescia, and Bergamo spent the summer there. To us it was simply home.

We lived six blocks south of the piazza. For generations the boys who lived on the plain, the "Flatlanders," had been locked in rivalry with the "Mountaineers," who lived on the hill. The first day I ventured out on the street I met Davolo and Gregorio, who were to become my best friends. They backed me up against a wall and inquired who I was and where I lived. When they learned that I was Gepetto's new son they broke into smiles and greeted me warmly. They informed me that I was a Flatlander, an eternal enemy of the Mountaineers; then they took me around to meet their gang.

The boys who lived in the lower town didn't care at all that I was made of wood: the only important thing was that I was a Flatlander, another fighter for their side. I learned to fight soon enough, and won the admiration of the pack when they saw how wooden punches raised bigger lumps than the most furious blows delivered by fists of flesh.

Flatlanders and Mountaineers observed an unwritten code of honor when they fought. I learned never to bite or scratch, hit a boy when he was down, or do lasting harm, and always to let an opponent go free when he grunted "Uncle." Father never scolded me for fighting, though he certainly would have let me have it if I had broken the rules: he had been a Flatlander himself.

School was neutral territory. Flatlanders and Mountaineers kept the peace at school, even on the playground. Father didn't send me to school right away. He wasn't rich, and couldn't afford to buy my books. He told me I would start school after my first birthday. By then he would have enough money for my books and I would have had a year to explore the world on my own terms. None of the Flatlanders had anything good to say about school, so I was glad enough to wait. Every day was full of adventure in the streets with my friends, and I paid no attention to the passing weeks and months. I lived for the moment, like every other boy I knew.

Father surprised me one morning when he announced that the next day would be my first birthday.

"We're going to have a big birthday party for you, Pinocchio. We'll eat at two o'clock. I'm preparing roast duck with hazelnut sauce, polenta, and truffles sauteed in butter, and Master Giuseppe is bringing the cake. Invite Davolo and Gregorio. I've carved wooden soldiers for them as gifts, and I have a surprise for you, too. You're going to have a wonderful first birthday party, my boy!"

I was very excited. I knew what birthday parties were like, for I had attended Davolo's party a month before. I rushed off to invite my friends.

When I returned home, I found that Giuseppe had already brought the cake. Where he got it I didn't know; it certainly was too splendid for any bakery in our little village. Four layers frosted in dark, rich chocolate—four layers! Frosting graced the sides in thick festoons and covered the top in intricate swirls. I had never seen such a magnificent, mouth-watering cake in my brief life, nor have I seen its like since.

Giuseppe looked at my bulging eyes and frowned. He dragged a chair over to the tall kitchen cabinet, climbed up on it with the cake, and carefully placed the cake on top of the cabinet.

"I'm putting your cake up here so you won't be tempted to sample it before the party, Pinocchio. A very bad thing will happen if you do. You must wait patiently till the party."

"I won't touch it, Master Giuseppe, believe me," I promised sincerely. I had no intention of spoiling my birthday cake; I wanted Davolo and Gregorio to see it in all its glory before we devoured it.

Chapter 4

I lay awake for a long time that night thinking of the fun we would have at my party. I dreamed of chocolate cake when I finally fell asleep, the very cake waiting for me in the next room.

I awoke early to find Father already up. After breakfast he called me to his side.

"The first thing we must do today, Pinocchio, is wind you up again. Take off your shirt."

I took off my shirt and Father turned the key twelve times. With each turn I grew stronger. By the time he finished with me I felt I could lick all the Mountaineers single-handedly. I hadn't realized how much my vigor had declined in a year.

Father went up the hill to have coffee with Giuseppe while I put on my shirt and ran out to find Davolo and Gregorio. We would play all morning and return to the house for the party.

By noon we were hungry, so we returned home to look for a bit of sausage and bread for lunch. I couldn't resist pointing out the cake.

"Just look at the cake Master Giuseppe brought for the party! Have you ever seen one like it? I'm sure such a wonderful cake has never been seen before in our village."

My friends stared silently, reverently, at the chocolate terraces that rose like a dark temple above the kitchen cabinet. Davolo voiced the thought that had risen in all our minds. "Pinocchio, the frosting looks so thick! Let's have a taste before the party. There's so much frosting that no one will ever notice if we each swipe a fingerlick. We can smooth it over with a knife."

"Master Giuseppe said something very bad would happen if I sampled the cake before the party," I protested weakly.

"What could happen? We won't eat enough to get sick, and we can smooth out the frosting so no one will know. It's not as though the cake is for someone else. It's for you, Pinocchio, you and your friends. That's what Master Giuseppe said, right?"

"Yes, that's true. And Father didn't tell me not to eat the cake; Giuseppe did, and he's not my father. We'll do it."

We pushed the table over to the cabinet and I, being tallest, climbed up on it. I couldn't quite reach the cake. Gregorio handed me the chair, which I put on top of the table. I carefully climbed up on the chair. I could easily reach the cake now. I handed it down to Gregorio, who had climbed up on the table, and Gregorio handed it to Davolo. Gregorio and I both climbed down. Davolo put the cake on the table.

We each took just one fingerlick. The sweet creamy chocolate taste was even more delicious than we had expected. We licked our lips with relish. How we would savor a whole slice of this masterpiece!

I got a knife from the kitchen cabinet and erased the three gashes we had made in the frosted surface. Perfect. No one would guess that we had tasted the frosting.

I climbed back on the chair and Gregorio climbed back on the table. Davolo handed the cake to Gregorio and he handed it on to me. I lifted the cake over my head to put it back on the kitchen cabinet.

Without warning the chair started to tip. I could do nothing as it slid out from under me. Down I crashed, right on Gregorio; and the cake fell on us both.

At that very moment Giuseppe and Father entered the kitchen.

Without warning the chair started to tip. I could do nothing as it slid out from under me. Down I crashed, right on Gregorio…

Chapter 5

For the longest minute in my life neither Father nor Giuseppe spoke. Disbelief and shame covered Father's face; Giuseppe frowned in somber silence.

"Pinocchio, look what you have done!" Father said at last. "After all Master Giuseppe has done for you, you have disregarded his warning. Worse, you disobeyed an elder. Your party is ruined and you have shamed me. What kind of father must he think me, who cannot train his child to obey one simple command?"

"It's not your fault, Gepetto," said Giuseppe, speaking at last. "Pinocchio fell to temptation, like a real boy. He does not know how great that fall was. We will talk later, Friend." With those words to Father, Giuseppe turned and left, without a word to me.

Father turned from the door and looked at me again, tears in his eyes. I was crying, too.

"Davolo made me do it, he and Gregorio," I blubbered. I looked around to find my partners in sin, but they were nowhere to be seen.

"Well," sighed Father, "you'll have to apologize to Master Giuseppe when his wrath has cooled. You know he loves you, Pinocchio. He's very disappointed in you; that's why he's angry.

"I'm angry, too, but I think you've been punished enough by the loss of your cake and party. Let's get you cleaned up. You're filthy with that chocolate all over you. Take off your clothes, and into the tub with you."

A large kettle of water always sat steaming on the stove, for Father never knew when a visitor might drop in for coffee. He poured all the hot water into the tub and added more water from the well while I took off my clothes. I climbed into the tub and Father tossed me a large cake of lye soap and a stiff brush. I began to scrub while Father busied himself cleaning my clothes.

Father had no trouble washing the chocolate out of my clothes, but try as I might I couldn't scrub my body clean. Most of the chocolate came off, but faint, dark stains continued to appear on my hands after every lathering and rinsing. Father came to help scrub me, but he also was unable to wash the brown spots from my hands.

"This is very strange, son. The clothes came clean, but your wooden hands, which have no pores, are stained. I don't understand...." Father didn't finish his sentence; instead, he gasped with horror.

"Your key! Where is your key?"

I looked over my shoulder into the mirror behind me. My key was gone! The keyhole was empty; no, not empty, but filled with dried, caked chocolate.

"The key must have popped out when I fell, Father."

We searched carefully through all the crumbs and chocolate covering the floor. I went through all my clothing while Father swept the room thoroughly. We both took a candle in hand and got down on hands and knees to examine every inch of the floor. We even sifted through the ashes in the fireplace. It was no use; the key could not be found. The only thing I saw on the floor that didn't belong there was a black cricket crouching on the hearth. In anger and frustration I threw my shoe at it, but the insect sprang up into the chimney.

Father had calmed down. "Tomorrow, when you go to apologize to Master Giuseppe, we'll ask him to make you a new key. It could take a while. How fortunate that I wound you up this morning. That seems to be the only thing that went right today."

I began to cry again. "Father, I'm so sorry. I disobeyed and brought shame on you as well as myself. I feel very miserable."

Father put his arms around me.

"If you were a real boy, you would disobey and shame me many times growing up. I forgive you. Tomorrow we'll make up with Master Giuseppe and take care of the key problem. But it's very strange that the key is nowhere to be found. Maybe one of your fine friends scampered off with it."

Father's suggestion struck me as a likely explanation of the missing key. I ran first to Davolo's house to see if he had picked it up. I grabbed the cord and rang the bell vigorously. No one answered, but I heard a rustling inside. I banged on the door with my wooden fists and called to my friend.

"Open up, Davolo, I know you're there," I said loudly. The door opened a crack. From the darkness inside a frightened voice said, "What do you want?"

"Don't be afraid, Davolo; I'm not angry. You tempted me, but it was my fault I gave in. I wanted the chocolate as much as you did. I came to see if you picked up a key from the floor before you took off. The key Father winds me with came out when I fell. Did you take it?"

Davolo opened the door fully. I could see that he was still shaken by our fall.

"No, Pinocchio, I didn't see your key. I saw only your father and Master Giuseppe. I just wanted to get out of there; I didn't pick up anything." Davolo spoke with such fear and sincerity that I had to believe him.

I went on to Gregorio's house. Signora Samsa answered the door before I knocked. She was agitated and began to speak before I could open my mouth.

"Pinocchio, where is my son? Gregorio said he was going to your party this morning. I haven't seen him since. I am so worried!"

"I don't know, Signora," I stammered. "We had a little accident before the party started. I thought he ran home, though I didn't actually see him leave. He hasn't been home at all?"

"No. Did he do something bad, something that might have landed him in trouble? Something he might run away for?"

"No, Signora," I answered; and I told her the whole story. "You know my father and Master Giuseppe, Signora," I concluded. "I'm sure Gregorio was scared; but he knows they wouldn't do anything more than tell you. You might give him a licking, but Gregorio's had plenty of lickings before. I can't believe he'd run away from a licking."

I left Gregorio's house wondering where he was and if he had my key. When I got home I found Father had heated up my birthday meal. I had no appetite and went straight to bed. I slept badly and awoke very early. I did not look forward to seeing Master Giuseppe.

Giuseppe received us gravely. He embraced Father, murmuring a greeting; then he turned and looked me straight in the eye. I blurted out an apology prompted more by fear than by remorse. I didn't honestly feel I had done wrong in sampling the cake. It was meant for me on my birthday and my birthday had arrived. If Giuseppe had really wanted to keep it from me till the hour of the party, he shouldn't have put it where I could get at it, or he should have put it in a box so it wouldn't tempt me. It was Giuseppe's fault, more than anyone's, that I tried the cake and fell into this mess. Of course I didn't speak frankly, but that was how I felt.

When I finished telling Giuseppe how sorry I was, he spoke to me for the first time since my fall.

"I forgive you, Pinocchio. As I said yesterday, you acted like any boy. But there is a price to be paid for that."

Giuseppe did not explain what he meant and I was afraid to ask. Father did not ask either, but brought up the matter of the key.

"Giuseppe, it seems that when Pinocchio fell his key popped out. Here, see the empty keyhole in his back."

I pulled up my shirt and Giuseppe silently examined the keyhole.

"We've searched the house inside out, from top to bottom," Father continued, "but we can't find the key. It's as though it vanished from the face of the earth. Giuseppe, would you make a new key for Pinocchio?"

Father and I were both shocked at Giuseppe's reply.

"I could make another key for Pinocchio, but it would be useless. You see, the keyhole is plugged with dried chocolate. It cannot be removed. Go ahead, Gepetto, try."

Father tried to ream out the keyhole with one of Giuseppe's awls. The chocolate was harder than stone. Father couldn't scrape out the smallest pinch of dust though he pressed the awl so hard that he turned the point. He looked at Giuseppe, amazed.

"That's not all, Gepetto. The stains on Pinocchio's hands come from within; that's why you can't wash them away. Some of the frosting got into Pinocchio's works and is now sealed inside his body. It can't be removed. The chocolate won't harden in there as it did in the keyhole, but it has coated all his gears. It will hinder his actions and muddle his thinking. All this is the price Pinocchio must pay for his disobedience."

Father was shaken by Giuseppe's words. "Don't tell me any more, Giuseppe," he cried with anguish. "Pinocchio is doomed! His brief life will be gummed up by the chocolate inside, and he will run down in a year. Oh, my friend, what are we to do? What are we

"Giuseppe, it seems that when Pinocchio fell his key popped out. Here, see the empty keyhole in his back."
I pulled up my shirt and Giuseppe silently examined the keyhole.

to do?" Father started to weep, and as I grasped what would happen to me I burst into tears, too.

Giuseppe interrupted us. "All is not hopeless. It's true that Pinocchio the wooden boy is doomed. But if he could become a real flesh-and-blood boy he could look forward to a life as long as yours."

"You and I make wonderful creations of wood," Father replied wryly, "but flesh and blood is a little out of our line. Do you propose an alliance with the butcher?"

"No," smiled Giuseppe. "But I have a plan. I can't reveal it now. Wait patiently; I'll set my plan in motion when its time has come."

Father managed a faint smile. "You didn't fail me when I asked you to help me create a life-like manikin, Giuseppe. I must trust you now. Pinocchio has no other hope."

I didn't share Father's great faith in Giuseppe, but I did share his fear of what would happen to me. I was only a year old, but I already knew what death was. Marco, one of the Mountaineers, had come down with scarlet fever and died a month before my birthday. All the boys in town, Flatlanders and Mountaineers, had gone to the funeral. As I shuffled past Marco's little casket and looked down at his still, bloodless face surrounded by white satin, I felt suddenly grateful that I would never die. No longer would Marco feel the warm sun, smell baking bread, run a race and win, and do the other things boys enjoy. That thought made death dreadful to me. I rejoiced then that I was made of wood and not frail flesh. Now death threatened to claim me, too.

I could see that Giuseppe was right: becoming a real boy was my only hope of escaping an early death. But how could a woodcarver, even the greatest in Italy, turn wood into flesh, blood, and bone?

Chapter 6

I didn't sleep at all that night, but by first light I had concocted my own plan for becoming a real boy. I ran to wake Father.

"Father, wake up! I have figured out how to become a real boy. You must enroll me in school this very morning. I want to begin studying as soon as possible."

Father had not slept either. His eyes were red from weeping, but he had to smile at my proposal.

"Son, the chocolate certainly has gummed up your brain. I never knew a boy who didn't think of school as death itself. You talk as though it were the key to life. Why are you so anxious to start school?"

"I must learn the secrets of nature, Father. If alchemists can learn how to turn base metal into gold, perhaps I can learn how to turn wood into flesh and blood."

Nearly everyone in our village, young and old alike, believed that alchemists really knew how to turn lead, tin, and copper into pure gold. Old Lazaro Paracelso, a beggar who lived in a shack in the woods above the village, was held by all the boys to be an alchemist. We were certain he had a hoard of doubloons cached in a nearby cave, gold coins created from the coppers he begged in the piazza. We had explored all the caves in the vicinity back to their farthest reaches without result, but failure had not shaken our opinion. I reasoned that if an old man like Lazaro could learn to turn lead into gold, I could learn to transform my wooden self into a regular boy.

Father was one of the few in our village who denied that alchemists could create gold. But he thought going to school would be better for me than wandering idly about town with my friends, so he agreed to my proposition.

"I think that's a good idea, Pinocchio. We'll enroll you today. I still believe Master Giuseppe will find a way to make you a real boy, but school is a good thing for now."

We walked to school after breakfast. Father enrolled me and paid for my books while I ran off to greet my friends on the playground. They were all there except Gregorio. No one knew where he was. There was talk he had run away from home. When the schoolmaster rang the bell, Father returned home and I entered the schoolhouse to begin life as a scholar.

My friends were not surprised to see me; they knew I would start school after my birthday. But they were amazed at my eagerness to learn. They had expected me to be more interested in mischief than books; and I would have been the chief clown, too, except that I never forgot I was studying for my life. In two weeks I was reading as well as any of them; in a month I led the class in arithmetic.

I was sorely tempted to join my comrades in their pranks, for our schoolmaster, Signor Pagliacci, was such a buffoon that he practically invited mischief. All the boys despised him. They didn't pay the least attention to his dry lectures, but used their wits to make trouble for him.

Signor Pagliacci's looks were ridiculous enough. Blotchy, yellow skin stretched tightly over a bulging, shiny dome and sagged loosely over a pinched, hairless face that tapered down to a weak double chin. To be fair to the man, I must say that our schoolmaster was not entirely without hair: his head sported a dozen or so yellow-white hairs, which he had grown out a foot long so he could comb them back and forth over his naked skull. His eyes were yellow, like his skin. Only his nose, a red, warty mass, broke the yellow monotony of his face. This magnificently comical head jutted forward on a scrawny neck attached to a body that must be described as a pot belly with arms and legs. The belly served to balance the head and keep the man from toppling over.

You would think a man cursed with such looks would do what he could to cover up—grow a bushy beard, wear loose clothes, or keep his hat on whenever he could. But our schoolmaster was so proud and conceited that he did none of these things. He thought himself handsome, clever, and charming, and made no effort to disguise his self-esteem.

The boys vied with each other in causing trouble for the schoolmaster. Davolo (whom we all called Daviolo, "Devil", for obvious reasons) was particularly skilled at disrupting class and making Signor Pagliacci look foolish without even realizing it.

Once Signor Pagliacci caught Davolo whispering to a boy named Alfredo. He snatched up his cane and advanced towards the pair, blustering and threatening.

Once Signor Pagliacci caught Davolo whispering to a boy named Alfredo. He snatched up his cane and advanced towards the pair, blustering and threatening.

"Whispering while I am talking, you good-for-nothings? You won't whisper when I've finished with you! Just what did you consider more important than my lecture on verbs?"

Davolo replied with a boldness that seemed to spring from complete innocence. "Sir, Alfredo was expressing his opinion that the most handsome feature of your noble profile is your high, intelligent forehead, while I was maintaining that your nose, so like that of the Caesars, ought most to be praised."

Signor Pagliacci blushed and stammered: "Well, I don't know; I suppose you both have a case; I, I...."

I could keep silent no longer: "No, Davolo and Alfredo are both idiots!" I cried out. "It is Signor Pagliacci's strong chin, thrust forward so bravely, that gives his face the classic Roman proportions we all admire."

The other lads were quick to catch on. Before Signor Pagliacci could get another word in all of us were loudly praising his eyes, ears, hair (what there was of it), double chin (so mature!), and even the mole on his cheek. We then began to shout insults at each other for favoring a different part of the poor schoolmaster's face. We finished with a splendid fist fight, every boy against every other boy (taking care to injure no one). Signor Pagliacci finally had to ring the bell to signal the end of the morning session and send us home for our midday meal.

It was another prank of Davolo's that brought an end to my brief career as a scholar. My friend had drawn a droll caricature of Signor Pagliacci's face. Below the drawing he had written the words, "The Man I Love. Carlo Pagliacci." By those words Davolo meant to indicate that our schoolmaster loved himself.

As Davolo's drawing made its way around the class the teacher heard our snickers and deftly snatched the cartoon from a boy named Luciano. His face reddened as he took in its obvious meaning. His hand shook with rage as he held it up before us.

"Who is responsible for this?" he bellowed.

Davolo spoke right up with that air of innocence he affected so well. "Sir, I brought that drawing to school. Just this morning Signorina Dolcinea dropped it as she entered church. I would have returned it to her on the spot, but I didn't want to be late for your most illuminating lectures. I'll return it to her on my way home today."

Now, you need to know that Signor Pagliacci was hopelessly in love with Signorina Dolcinea, whom he considered an angel in human form. Conceited as he was, he couldn't understand why she was cold and distant when he spoke to her. Signorina Dolcinea was no beauty, and was getting along in years, but she had too much good sense and dignity to be interested in a puffed up pipsqueak like Pagliacci.

When the schoolmaster heard Davolo's explanation, he smiled. "That's all right, Davolo," he genially replied. "I guess I misunderstood the words at the bottom of this precious likeness. You need not trouble to call on the lovely Signorina Dolcinea this afternoon; go play with your friends. I will return the sketch to her myself. Let us proceed with our lesson. No, perhaps we should take an early lunch. In fact, in honor of the king's birthday I shall declare the rest of the day a school holiday. You are dismissed."

We never saw Signor Pagliacci again. He called on the signorina that very afternoon. When she opened her door, he immediately showed her the caricature and openly declared that he loved her as much as she loved him. The shocked woman angrily insisted that he leave at once. Our teacher mistook her protests for coyness and continued to swear devotion to his beloved so loudly that the whole street rushed to their windows to take in the spectacle. Signorina Dolcinea called for her two brothers. They were brawny lads, devoted to their sister. Unlike the neighbors, they saw no humor in the situation; they fell upon Signor Pagliacci and beat him until he managed to escape. He fled up the street bruised, perplexed, and still unaware that Davolo had tricked him.

Signor Pagliacci was overwhelmed with humiliation. The story would be all over town by morning. He feared for his life if he should ever meet up with the brothers again. In our tiny village that would only be a matter of a very little time. Our schoolmaster packed his belongings and left for good before nightfall.

The village fathers were unable to secure another teacher for the remainder of the school year. I didn't regret it, for the very day Signor Pagliacci left I had come to realize that no amount of schooling would give me knowledge of how to become a real boy. I had been eagerly reading a book written by a professor at the university when the following words caused my heart to sink:

> The Law of Kinds is one of the most certain laws of nature. Every species reproduces its own kind. Frogs lay eggs that produce other frogs, not toads. Chimpanzees give birth to baby chimpanzees, not monkeys or gorillas. Human babies are begotten only by human parents.

The meaning for me was all too clear. The most learned scholars didn't know how to turn a flesh-and-blood animal like a frog into another flesh-and-blood animal, even one as similar as a toad. But surely that would be easier to do than turning a wooden boy into flesh and blood. Schooling had failed me. Where could I turn?

Chapter 7

I sat slumping at home for a week after Signor Pagliacci's disappearance. I told Father how crushed I was to learn that even the most learned professors could not turn a frog into a toad, much less a wooden boy into a real one.

Father was not surprised or distressed by this news, but he saw how near despair I was and tried to cheer me up. "We must wait for Master Giuseppe to tell us his plan. He has been my best friend for years and has never failed me yet."

"Father, that's easier for you to believe than for me," I replied. "Perhaps it's the chocolate gumming up my brain, but I can't be so confident. I wish I could."

That night I lay in bed trying to think of another plan, but nothing came. After an hour I began to drift off. Then something came to me in my half-awake state: a tiny voice calling my name! I sat up and tried to shake the chocolate out of my brain. There it was again, a real voice, much too high and small for Father.

I lit a candle and went to the door. Looking out on the street I saw only darkness. I shut the door and turned back to the room. Not another living soul was there except Father, who was sleeping soundly, and the cricket I had seen on my birthday. Anger flared up inside me as I remembered that fateful day. I threw my shoe at the cricket again, and once more it sprang up into the chimney. The voice did not return. I lay down in bed again and fell asleep after tossing unhappily for an hour.

I awoke the next morning tired and out of sorts. As I poked at my breakfast I watched Father working at his bench. He was finishing a bust of the king. With sure hands and unsurpassed art he had shaped a block of wood into a noble head worthy to be compared to the most exalted of European monarchs. From his imperial crown to his strong cleft chin, our wooden sovereign looked destined to restore Italy to the greatness she knew under the Caesars. Yet Father had carved the bust out of pine, the most common of woods. Father talked to me as he worked.

"I use pine, son, because the village council can't afford anything better. But it won't make any difference in the long run. After I paint the king no one will know what kind of wood lies underneath. I will turn this pine crown into glittering gold. Not like old Lazaro, of course; he can do the real thing, eh?"

Father's remark started me thinking. Respected scholars could not turn one animal into another, but alchemists could turn copper into gold; so I believed with all my heart. If they could do that with their secret powers, perhaps they could show me how to turn my wooden body into hair, skin, flesh, and bones. I would visit Lazaro Paracelso immediately.

It was early spring and the air was still quite cold, for a chilly wind was blowing down from the Alps. Even wooden boys get cold, so I put on two shirts and a cap and went down to the piazza, hoping to find Lazaro on his usual corner. The old beggar was not there, no doubt because it was so cold out in the open. I turned around and began walking briskly up the hill towards his shack.

Lazaro's hut was hidden in a grove of quince bushes about a stone's throw from the road. Even in the spring, when the quince branches were gray and bare, the hut could not be seen from the road. It was just as well that Lazaro's dwelling lay out of sight, for it could only be called a hovel. The thatch roof was black and rotten, and empty knotholes gaped in the rough planks that served as walls.

I knocked boldly on the door: hope had chased away my fears. Lazaro opened the door a crack, so as not to let in any more cold air than necessary. He silently looked me up and down.

"Who are you, young man, and why have you come to visit an old beggar?" he asked. "Perhaps you wish to give alms to a poor but deserving old man so he can buy firewood?"

"My name is Pinocchio, Signor. My father is Gepetto the woodcarver; surely you know him. I have no alms to give, Signor, for we are not wealthy, but I have come to offer you my service in exchange for your knowledge."

"What service can you offer me, and what knowledge can I give you?" Lazaro asked in reply. "I am a poor beggar, injured in battle while faithfully serving my king. A beggar doesn't need a servant. If the good people of our village knew I had a servant they might think I had more money than I need. And what knowledge do I have except bitter knowledge, from my own wretched experience, of the greed and hardness of human hearts?"

"Signor, I know you are skilled in alchemy. I wish to learn your secrets. I don't wish to learn all of them, no, not at all. I don't care about turning lead or copper into gold. What I want to know is how to turn wood into flesh and blood. You must have heard that I am a wooden boy. I long to become a real boy. If you can turn base metal into gold, you must be able to turn wood into flesh and blood."

The wind from the mountains blew harder. Lazaro looked left and right and down the path leading to the road. "Are you alone, Pinocchio?" he asked.

"Yes," I replied. "When I got my brainstorm of how you could help me—and of how I might be of service to you," I hastily added, "I came here right away. Even Father doesn't know where I am."

Lazaro smiled just the way he would smile when greeting a fine gentleman or lady in the piazza. "Please come in, young Pinocchio," he said pleasantly. "I accept your offer. You will serve me, and I will transform you."

I entered the dark little hut with a heart full of excitement. As soon as he had shut the door, Lazaro grabbed my arm.

"What are you doing?" I cried.

"Why, young fool, you're going to serve me, and I'm going to transform you, all at the same time. I'm going to turn you into smoke and ashes. The cold weather has made this a bad week for begging. I've been unable to buy both food and firewood. You shall be my firewood."

"But one of your many pieces of gold would buy a whole cart-load of firewood, cut and stacked against the side of your house," I protested. "You must have many chests of gold."

"Do you really believe I am an alchemist?" Lazaro asked scornfully. "I once followed that road; I found that it leads only to poverty. Oh yes, we alchemists transform one substance into another: we turn our money into air and decent clothing into rags; we transform ourselves from respectable men into beggars. If anyone tells you otherwise he is a liar. You think we have magical powers? Perhaps we do. Magic is dark, and I can't afford even a tallow candle to light this miserable shack. But tonight I will be warm and have light when you are crackling brightly on my hearth. Many thanks for your service."

"But one of your many pieces of gold would buy a whole cartload of firewood, cut and stacked against the side of your house," I protested. "You must have many chests of gold."

I wanted to cry out for help, but I knew no one would be near Lazaro's hut in the middle of the morning. It would have been useless to struggle, for Lazaro continued to grip me with his dirty, wiry hand like a varmint trap grips a weasel. I was strong for a boy, but no match for that wicked beggar. Squatting on the cobblestones in the piazza, his greasy hat lying upturned in front of him to receive alms, Lazaro looked skinny and frail, as though a gust of wind would blow him across the square like a dry leaf. Now I knew better. I would have to think fast if I wanted to live past nightfall.

"Well, Signor, I know you won't burn me till it gets dark, since you want the benefit of my light as well as my heat. May I ask a favor of you? I'd like to eat some fruit from the wild quince growing around your house as a last meal."

"Eat the fruit of the wild quince? They're too sour for anything but jam, and even then a cook must mix a great deal of honey in with them." He eyed me intently beneath lowered brows. "Just why do you want to eat them? Tell me the truth."

I collapsed on the floor and began to cry. "I was afraid you would be suspicious, Signor. The truth is, they are very special quinces. My teacher, Signor Pagliacci, told me that quince fruit that remains on the bush all winter is wisdom fruit. He said that those who eat of it will find it sweet to the taste and will grow wise. Everyone thinks Signor Pagliacci left town in shame and fear; but in fact he left to take up an appointment at the university. I confess, Signor, that I hoped eating your quinces would make me clever enough to find a way to escape; but you were too smart for me."

"You believed that old buffoon?" Lazaro laughed. "I told you, there is no magic power in anything, not in alchemical elixirs and certainly not in wild quince fruit. What a little fool you are!"

Lazaro sat down on the only stool in the hut and fell silent. I knew he was brooding on what I had said. After a while he locked me in the hut and went outside. I ran to the wall and peeked through a knothole. There he was, gorging on the small yellow fruit growing outside his shack, just as I hoped he would. The greedy old beggar ate till his mouth was so puckered he couldn't open it. His face told me he didn't find the fruit of the wild quince sweet. Then he doubled over with stomach pains and fell on the ground, writhing and whimpering in pain.

While Lazaro rolled around helplessly on the ground, I looked for a way to break out of the hut. Finding no tool to force the door, I kicked at it till it shattered into splinters. As I left the beggar's shack, I jeered at him.

"Who's the gullible one now? There's no fool like an old fool. You threw your life away pursuing dark secrets, yet you jumped at the chance to obtain hidden wisdom by stuffing yourself with wild quince. You're as big a fool as our late conceited schoolmaster. Why, I know more than you both, and my wooden brain is addled with chocolate."

Lazaro groaned, but I couldn't make out what he said and didn't care. I headed back to the village, puffed up with pride that I had escaped from that clever rogue by using my wits. But by the time I reached Father and sat down to supper I was near despair again. I still didn't know how to become a real boy, and only eight months remained till I ran down.

Chapter 8

The following morning Father told me that Barbe Filippo would be paying a visit.

Did I mention that Father was a Waldense? The Waldenses are a church of plain Christians who have lived in the valleys of the Alps for centuries. They hold to the simple Gospel and shun tradition and ceremony. They call one another *Brother* and address their ministers as *Barbe*, or *Uncle*.

Barbe Filippo was the Waldensian minister in our village. His was a face to inspire confidence (a great help to a minister). He had moist, bright gray eyes, a full head of wavy brown hair, and a reddish-brown mustache that turned up because he waxed it. When Barbe smiled—and he smiled readily—he revealed fine white teeth. He wore a small goatee, which was the same color as his mustache. Barbe was of medium build, muscular and hardened by blacksmithing, his week-day trade. Everyone in the village, Catholics as well as Waldenses, admired him as a man's man and a faithful minister of God.

Barbe Filippo was Father's cousin on his mother's side. Father was always joking that his family relations were so mixed up that his cousin was his uncle. Whenever Father said this, Barbe Filippo would reply that his family relations were equally confused: his cousin was his brother. The villagers would laugh every time they heard this exchange, not because it was really funny anymore but because they were so fond of both men.

Father took me to church from the beginning. Since I was not a real boy, I could not be baptized. That made Barbe Filippo's visit difficult. He had heard how low Father had become after my fall and was coming to offer spiritual encouragement; but what hope could he hold out for me?

Barbe appeared at the door wearing his usual friendly smile. The men embraced with a traditional abraccio and went into the kitchen to sit and talk. I sat on the hearth and leaned back against the chimney to listen. After Father had poured mugs of steaming coffee for himself and his guest, Barbe began to speak. His voice was steady, but his words vibrated with his concern.

"Gepetto, I worry about what I hear. People say gloom is your constant companion now. You've been a Christian too long to be a prisoner of despair."

"Gepetto, I worry about what I hear. People say gloom is your constant companion now. You've been a Christian too long to be a prisoner of despair."

"Oh no, Filippo," Father replied with a faint smile, "I don't despair. My hope of eternal life still rests firmly in Christ. I confess I fell into deep darkness of soul when Giuseppe told me Pinocchio couldn't be wound up again. But he assured me he has a plan to turn Pinocchio into a real boy. I have great faith in Giuseppe, Filippo, but sometimes my confidence falters. At such times I get very sad for Pinocchio; but for myself, no, I don't despair."

Barbe Filippo relaxed. "You've relieved my mind, Brother. The state of your soul was my chief concern. I was going to exhort you to let your love for Pinocchio be like our love for a puppy. We love our pets, knowing all the while that when they die they are no more. The knowledge they will die someday does not fill us with despair, though we weep when we lose them; for they face neither heaven nor hell.

"But now you tell me Brother Giuseppe has a plan to transform Pinocchio into a real boy. That puts things in a new light. If Pinocchio became a flesh-and-blood boy, a child of Adam, he could become a believer; he could be born again as a child of God. Let us ask God to give Brother Giuseppe success."

Barbe Filippo and Father prayed right there that Giuseppe would be able to turn me into a real boy. I bowed my head in respect. I *hoped* God would answer their prayers, but in my wooden, chocolate-soaked heart I knew that I had no real faith in Giuseppe or in the Lord.

Barbe stayed to finish his coffee and talk of other things with Father. I excused myself and went out to find my friends. We walked around the village, bored and restless; then we swaggered up the hill looking for a fight. We didn't sight a single Mountaineer, but none of us really cared. The prospect of rolling around in the dust punching and kicking our rivals didn't stir us as it had when Gregorio led our gang. We all missed Gregorio. He would have cooked up some interesting mischief for us, but he had been gone four months. No one had seen him or heard a word about him.

We wandered aimlessly through the lanes of the upper village for an hour or so, then tramped back to the piazza, peevish and out of sorts. Unable to think of anything better to do, one by one we all drifted off home.

As I lay in bed that night feeling sorry for myself I again heard that tiny voice call my name.

"Pinocchio! Pinocchio! Look over on the hearth."

I hurriedly lit a candle and approached the fireplace. I saw nothing. Oh yes, there was that cricket again. This time it was jumping up and down, squeaking the way crickets do. No, it was not squeaking the way crickets do: those squeaks were words! The cricket was calling my name!

I sat down beside the insect, moving slowly so as not to frighten it.

"Is it really you, cricket, calling me?" I whispered. I didn't want Father to hear me. He would never believe me if I told him I was talking to a cricket. But Father snored on softly.

"Yes, Pinocchio, it is I," the cricket answered. "Don't be amazed that I can talk. I learned to talk at my mother's knee. Pinocchio, I am Gregorio!"

"Gregorio? My friend, Gregorio Samsa?" I held out my hand and the cricket sprang onto the open palm. I carefully placed the insect on my shoulder so I could hear it better.

"Tell me what happened to you, Gregorio, and where you have been all this time," I whispered.

"I have been right here in your house ever since we fell with your cake. I was knocked unconscious for a moment and awoke to find I had been transformed into a large insect. Then I saw the boots of your father and Master Giuseppe bearing down on me and I leaped for the safety of the hearth. Here I have lived these past four months, eating crumbs, trying to speak to you, and dodging your shoes."

"I'm sorry about the shoes," I replied, "but put yourself in my place and you'll understand my feelings when I saw you. I must know, Gregorio: How did you turn into an insect?"

"Until today I didn't understand my metamorphosis," the cricket said. "When I saw myself in the mirror I couldn't doubt that I was an insect, but I was at a loss to explain how the change came about. Only when I heard Barbe Filippo talking did I grasp why I had become a cricket."

"Barbe said nothing about crickets."

"No; but he said that you, Pinocchio, were like an animal that simply ceases to be when it dies. A faithful hound doesn't inherit heaven; a vicious cur doesn't go to hell. An animal has no idea that eternal happiness or eternal suffering awaits any living creature. Well, that was just my frame of mind when we stole a taste of frosting. I didn't believe being good would bring me a heavenly reward, nor did I fear I would have to account to God for all my foolish deeds. I lived as if this life were all there is, the same as any animal. In my fall I took on the outward form of what I really am, a mere insect."

"Well, you certainly misunderstood Barbe," I replied. "That's not what he believes at all; I've been to church enough to know that. He teaches that human beings are made in God's image; that their race—your race, Gregorio—has fallen into sin; and that sinful human beings can be saved from sin and death and become children of God."

It seemed to me that Gregorio squeaked with anguish as he replied. "I would like to believe that I'm more than an insect, Pinocchio; I would like to believe that I'm a flesh-and-blood boy just having a dream about being an insect. But I know better when I see my shiny black body with wings, six legs, and two antennae. And when I see the lowly, wretched, vile creature I've become, I see myself with a hundred eyes. You can't imagine how depressing it is to see my loathsome form multiplied a hundredfold!"

I had to admit that Gregorio was an insect now. I could see it with my two eyes as well as he could with his hundred. I tried to cheer him up.

"Listen, Gregorio. If we can find a way for me to become a flesh-and-blood boy, we ought to be able to find a way for you to become a real boy again, too. We can talk to Barbe Filippo about becoming children of God once we're human, but first we must become human. Master Giuseppe said he had a plan, but he has said nothing about it now for four months. I think he was just trying to make Father and me feel better; I don't think he has a plan at all."

As I sat whispering to Gregorio in the dark, a plan of my own started to form in my mind. I continued, my excitement growing.

"Gregorio, I have a brilliant idea! Let's set out together and search the world for a way to become real boys. For you to remain here is to eat crumbs from the floor till someone finally squashes you flat. For me to remain here is to run down and come to a stop. We must leave the village and venture into the wide world. To stay where we are is to die. What do you say? Will you come with me?"

"You reason well for a manikin whose brain is clogged with chocolate," Gregorio squeaked. "I don't need any more convincing; I'm ready to leave at once. But what road will we take? What dangers will we meet with on the way? How will we know when we have found the secret of becoming human?"

"I don't know the answers to any of your questions, Gregorio. Let's talk tomorrow when I'm not so tired."

The next day I wove some willow branches into a traveling cage for Gregorio and tied it onto the end of a short pole. Father was amused that I had made a pet of the cricket. I didn't tell him the cricket on the hearth was Gregorio, nor did I tell him I intended to leave the village on a quest for life. I loved Father and didn't want to cause him more grief. I would write a note for him to find after I was gone; it would explain everything. Little did I realize how unloving my plan was at the time, nor how much grief it would cause my father.

Chapter 9

We could not leave on our quest without some money for the road. Gregorio suggested I sell my schoolbooks. I agreed; I had no reason to keep them. If I succeeded in my quest I would have plenty of time to earn money for new books; if I failed they would do me no good in the woodpile or the grave, wherever I wound up. I couldn't sell my books in the village; Father would hear of it. Besides, nobody would want to buy them now that our school was closed. I would sell them in a neighboring town where no one knew me.

The very next day I set out, Gregorio's cage and my books slung over my back, making for Romagnano, a market town south of our village. From Romagnano a road follows the Sesia River down to Casale, where the Sesia joins the Po. From there the southern road goes on to Genoa by way of Alessandria and Novi. In Genoa we could find a ship to take us anywhere in the world. We had no idea, of course, where in the world we should go once we reached Genoa. That's the problem with a brain addled by chocolate: it doesn't see far enough ahead. Gregorio didn't see the great flaw in the scheme either. I suppose that's to be expected in insects: they're all intuition and no reasoning, or so I've been told.

We didn't plan to proceed immediately to Genoa after selling my books. I would have to return home for a day or two. I had not yet composed my letter to Father. And I had not said goodbye to Gabriela.

Gabriela was an angel; that was the only word for her. She was the prettiest girl in the village, with raven-black hair, fair skin, and eyes as blue as Lake d'Orta. All the boys in the village were in love with Gabriela because she was so beautiful; but it was her sweet kindness and purity that made me adore her. I know you're supposed to adore God alone, and of course I didn't actually worship Gabriela, but I was convinced that she was more than human: she had to be an angel. Master Giuseppe had done his work well. Even with chocolate in my head I could feel love like a real boy.

Gabriela knew me only as a friend. I had to tell her how I felt about her before I left on my quest. Out of pure goodness she would pray for me and think of me, and whenever I remembered that, I would be strengthened and cheered on my way. Perhaps she would even love me and wait for me to return to her, as lovers do.

All went well our first day on the road. It was only April, but the weather was bright and sunny. The brown fields around us were showing a hint of green, the light breeze was soft and warm, and the scattered, fluffy clouds belonged more to early summer than to spring. Both of us were in high spirits, Gregorio chirping lustily.

By mid-morning we reached Romagnano. The piazza was four times as large as our own. Already a good crowd of townspeople had gathered there to buy, sell, or simply soak up the spring sunshine. I didn't have to stand in the square more than a quarter of an hour before a travelling peddler stopped to examine the books I had spread out on the cobblestones at my feet. We dickered a bit, and soon he was walking away with the books while I was showing Gregorio the money I had received.

"Look, Gregorio! Seven lire! I have never seen this much money in my life! We've enough to live on for two weeks at least. It's only one week to Genoa, so we'll have money for another week. By then surely we'll find someone who can show us how to become real boys."

"Well, I don't need money in my present state, that's for sure," Gregorio replied. "Anywhere crumbs have been dropped is a fine place for me to dine."

We started back home. As I strode along, Gregorio swinging behind my back, we came upon two men going in the same direction, whom I recognized as a pair of vagabonds I had seen in the piazza.

They were an odd pair. The taller one looked very much like a fox. A shock of stiff red hair topped his head and large pointed ears poked up on both sides of his crown, while his narrow face tapered out into a long nose. His black eyes darted back and forth unceasingly. The shorter, plumper man reminded me at once of our neighbor's cat. His yellow-green eyes stared vacantly from a puffy face covered with soft gray whiskers, and a flat, pink tongue constantly licked his lips. The tall man leaned on his shorter companion for support even as he directed his steps along the road. I concluded that the foxy man must be lame and his friend blind.

They were an odd pair. The taller one looked very much like a fox. The shorter, plumper man reminded me at once of our neighbor's cat. His yellow-green eyes stared vacantly from a puffy face....

The lame man greeted me as I drew abreast of them. His voice was rich and warm, and I immediately sensed that he was a man who could be trusted.

"Good morning, young Signor. Permit me to introduce myself and my companion. I am Signor Volpe and this is Signor Gatto. I can see that you are a gentleman of breeding and intelligence, the kind of person Signor Gatto and I should like to converse with on the road. Where are you headed this fine day?"

"Good morning to you, too, Signori," I replied politely. "My name is Pinocchio, and I am returning to my home, which is located in the next village. I cannot tell you its name, for it is so small that it does not have one. Didn't I notice you gentlemen in the piazza back in Romagnano?"

"Yes; how observant you are! We saw you there also, selling books. No doubt a shrewd young man of the world like you made a fine profit from the sale."

"Well, I did talk that stupid peddler out of seven copper lire; pretty good, if I do say so myself." I later discovered that I had sold my books for a pitifully small sum in light of their real worth, but in my innocence I was proud of my first business deal.

Signor Volpe, who spoke for both of them, praised me greatly for driving such a hard bargain and continued questioning me.

"No doubt you intend to invest your money and multiply it a hundredfold by sharp dealing, yes?"

"No, it is travelling money," I replied. "I am, as you may have noticed, a wooden boy. I am setting out on a quest to find the means of becoming a real boy."

"How fortunate that you have fallen in with us!" Signor Volpe replied with a smile. "We know just the man who can show you how to attain your goal. Isn't that right, Felice?"

"Yes, we know the man you seek," purred Signor Gatto.

"Why, that's wonderful!" I exclaimed. "I should be indebted to you all my life if you would direct me to him."

"The man is the famous Doctor Moro," the foxy man explained. "He lives on an island not far from Genoa. There he carries out just the sort of transformations you seek. I know in my heart that you are a discreet young gentleman, so I will tell you a secret, in strictest confidence, of course."

"Of course," I replied, eager to hear the secret.

"Signor Gatto and I were not always as you see us today," Signor Volpe confided. "Before Doctor Moro transformed us into men I was a fox and Signor Gatto was a cat. Can you believe it, looking at us now? Doctor Moro can do for you what he did for us."

It did not seem to me that Doctor Moro had done a complete job on Volpe and Gatto, but my time was running short and I was ready to clutch at any straw.

"Do you really think he could turn me into a flesh-and-blood boy?" I asked. Gregorio began to jump and chirp frantically at my side, and I hastened to inquire further, "Could he transform my pet cricket into a human being?"

"Oh yes; he is a wonder. But he charges a large fee for his services."

My hope withered as quickly as it had sprung up. "I have only these seven lire, and no means of gaining more!"

Signor Volpe smiled broadly, revealing teeth that were much too long and sharp for a normal man. The teeth didn't alarm me, for his words were smooth and honeyed.

"Ah, do not worry! Signor Gatto and I know how you can multiply your few copper coins into baskets of gold ducats, enough to pay the doctor and leave you with a fortune besides."

Now, you might think that I would have smelled a rat by this time, but you would be wrong. Signor Volpe was so flattering, and I wanted so to believe what he told me, that I threw caution to the winds. I had duped Lazaro Paracelso; now I was being duped. I eagerly pressed Signor Volpe to tell me how I could multiply my coppers into gold, and he was only too willing to do me this favor.

"Not far from here is a very special place called the Field of Wishes. In the middle of the field is a tree. You must bury your lire at the foot of the tree and make a wish that each coin will be turned into a basket of gold ducats. Then go away and return the next day. When you dig up your coins you will find your wishes have been granted."

"All your wishes, granted at once! Baskets of gold!" cried Signor Gatto.

"Where is the Field of Wishes?" I asked, hardly able to contain my excitement.

"Why, what luck!" exclaimed Signor Volpe. "It is right here, on our left."

Chapter 9

Next to the road lay a field of unplowed stubble. In the center of the field, a hundred yards from the road, stood a lone poplar tree. I turned to the men in gratitude.

"You must allow me to reward you with some of the gold when it is in my possession," I said.

"Oh no, we want nothing for ourselves," Signor Volpe protested with a smile. "We are already wealthy. The rags we wear are simply to fool robbers who might be lurking on the roads. Knowing that we have given you the means of becoming a real boy is happiness enough for us, right, Felice?"

"Yes, Rinardo, it is happiness enough for us."

I clambered over the low stone wall surrounding the field and began to run towards the tree. "Remember, you must not be found anywhere near the field tonight," Signor Volpe shouted after me. "Come back tomorrow and you will find baskets of gold. Goodbye, young friend; Signor Gatto and I must continue on our journey."

I was too caught up in thoughts of gold to bid them farewell. As I bent down by the tree and scooped a hole in the earth with my hands, I glanced up and saw the two men still there, peering at us over the wall. I carefully covered my coins with dirt and looked up again. Signor Volpe and Signor Gatto were not to be seen.

"What luck, Gregorio!" I said as I climbed over the wall and returned to the road. "We will be able to visit Doctor Moro after we have collected our treasure."

Gregorio had bounced and jounced mightily as I stumbled over the furrows towards the poplar tree and was too shaken up to reply for a minute or two. When he finally spoke my friend was still agitated, but not by his bumpy ride.

"Pinocchio, there was something about those men I didn't like. They were too much like animals to be human."

"Gregorio, you used to be human and now you are an animal. A cricket is even lower than a fox or cat. I trust you; why not them? They didn't even want any gold!"

"They were animals pretending to be human; I'm an animal that knows he's not human. There's a big difference. I tell you, something is not right. Didn't you see how they watched us from the other side of the wall? Think how suddenly they disappeared. I don't think Gatto is blind or Volpe lame. Do you know what I think? I think they want your money."

My friend's words would have made sense to anyone but a puppet who was not thinking clearly, which is just what I was. But I thought it was Gregorio who couldn't think clearly because he had been shaken up, and I didn't heed his warning.

We hurried home, arriving shortly before supper. Father asked me where I had been, and I told him that I had been out walking all day. My words were true as far as they went, but I was not telling the whole truth. This was the first time I had told a lie to Father. My nose tingled as I answered him.

Chapter 10

Gregorio and I slipped out of the house as soon as there was light enough for me to walk on the road without breaking my neck. In fact I did not walk, but ran down the empty road as fast as my wooden legs could go. I reached the field with the lone poplar just as the grayish-pink dawn had given way to the risen sun. I jumped over the wall and ran through the stubble towards the tall green form that stood guard over our treasure.

When I reached the foot of the tree, I saw a hole in the earth right where I had buried the seven lire! I dug frantically, knowing already what I would find—or not find, as the case was. I sifted through soil and rock until all hope had slipped away. My heart was leaden as I turned to Gregorio.

"You were right, Gregorio. There is nothing in this hole but worms. Volpe and Gatto are cheats. I let myself be deceived. Now what will we do?"

"We have to push on to Genoa, Pinocchio. We must go on even if we have to sleep in barns and suck raw eggs from henhouses. We may not know what lies ahead on the road, but if we go home we return only to die. Besides, we did not see Volpe and Gatto on the road this morning.

"They must have turned around and headed for Genoa themselves. Maybe we can track them down and recover your money."

I had to agree: "It seems we have no other choice. But we must go home for a day so I can write a note to Father and say goodbye to Gabriela."

We trudged back to the village. The morning was even lovelier than the day before, but we were too dejected to appreciate it.

I went first to see Gabriela. I wanted to give her a present in token of my love, but I had nothing. I was walking slowly down the street towards her house, wondering what I could do to impress her with my devotion and despairing of my situation, when I came upon the garden of Signora Fiore.

Signora Fiore's garden was the envy of all the village women. From early spring until the first frost of autumn, lovely flowers overflowed her whole yard from the low wall by the street all the way back to the house. I stopped by the wall and looked at the garden. Even in April it was alive with color and warmth.

You know already what I was thinking, don't you? I would pick a bouquet for the girl I loved. It was wrong, of course, to pick the flowers of Signora Fiore; but I told myself that she had more flowers than she needed. The old woman would not even miss those I was going to pick. That bouquet would bring me more happiness than it would ever bring her. I found it very easy to convince myself I was doing no wrong, so I picked almond blossoms, violets, jasmine, a little of everything I found in flower. Arms filled with blooms, I arrived at Gabriela's house and rapped on the door with my wooden nose. Gabriela gaped at me wide-eyed when she opened the door and saw me standing there. I started talking at once, before she could greet me; I was afraid I would be tongue-tied if she spoke first.

"Gabriela, I am leaving the village today to become a real boy, though I don't yet know how. I want you to know that I love you, that I have loved you since the day I first saw you. I hope you will wait for me to return as a real boy. Then perhaps I can court you and win your love. As a token of my love I bring these flowers, which I bought in the market this morning. They cost me my last lira, but I was glad to spend it on you. Will you accept them as the offering of a true and sincere heart?"

Gabriela flushed and said nothing. I thrust the flowers into her hands. As soon as she touched them she gasped and dropped them. She held up her hands and looked at them with horror: they were stained with chocolate! I looked down at the flowers and saw that the stems were covered with the dark brown liquid; I looked at my own hands and saw chocolate oozing from the pores.

"Dearest Gabriela," I cried miserably, "Please don't turn away from me! It's my sin, seeping out from inside, that you see; but I really do love you. I confess: I stole the flowers from the garden of Signora Fiore; but it was out of love for you. Please forgive me for giving you this terrible shock. I want you to love me. If you can't love me, please pray for me that I will become a real boy before I run down."

Gabriela had regained her composure. She didn't slam the door as I expected, but continued to stand there silently, pity and bewilderment on her face. I saw that I would have to tell her the whole story of my creation, fall, and quest. I told my tale as briefly as possible. When I had finished, Gabriela spoke for the first time.

I thrust the flowers into her hands. As soon as she touched them she gasped and dropped them. She held up her hands and looked at them with horror: they were stained with chocolate!

"Pinocchio, I want you to know that I do love you as a sister. Whether I can love you any other way, I don't know. You can be sure that I will pray for you and help you any way I can. Right now you must come in the house and let me wash that horrible chocolate off your hands. Unfortunately, I don't think I can do anything about your nose."

"My nose? What do you mean, my nose?" I asked, alarmed. I felt my nose, pulling my hand away immediately when I realized I had smeared chocolate on it. Brief as it was, that touch told me my nose was longer.

"Why, your nose has grown an inch just in the time you declared your love to me and gave me the flowers. Didn't you know?"

"No, not until I touched it just now," I answered. "But my nose tingled last night when I talked to Father. What could have made it grow?"

"I believe that telling lies caused your nose to grow longer," Gabriela explained. "Our lies are always obvious to everyone else: as the saying goes, they're as plain as the nose on your face."

"Then you knew even as I was speaking that I didn't buy the flowers in the market?"

"Certainly. A boy can't deceive a girl unless she allows herself to be deceived. But I also know your love for me is real. Come in, let me wash you."

I returned home that evening clean, but with an extra inch of nose. Father noticed it.

"Pinocchio, it's very strange, but I'm certain your nose is longer than it was when I carved it."

He sat me down by the candle and peered closely at my face. "Yes, it's definitely longer, at least an inch. Do you know what caused this?"

"No...I mean, yes, I think so," I said, correcting myself. I didn't want it to grow longer while talking to Father! "It seems to grow longer whenever I...well, whenever I...when I tell a lie."

"I can carve the extra wood off, son, but that won't change you inside. Maybe I should leave your nose as it is as a constant reminder to you of the state of your heart. I'll sleep on it. Which reminds me, it's after your bedtime."

When we were both in bed and the candle had been blown out, Father spoke to me in the darkness.

"What are you going to do tomorrow? Master Giuseppe told me today that the time is nearly here to put his plan into effect. Why don't you go up the hill and ask him if there's anything you can do to be ready for him when he comes to accomplish this great change?"

"Yes, Father," I lied, "That's just what I'll do tomorrow morning." I was glad it was dark so Father couldn't see that my nose had grown another half inch.

After Father fell asleep, I rose softly, crept into the kitchen, and lit a single candle. By its light I wrote my farewell letter. I told Father I was going out into the world to seek someone or something that could make me a real boy. I didn't tell him the road we would take, for I feared he would track me down and bring me back to be cured by Master Giuseppe.

Giuseppe had not spoken to us in several months. Strange as it seems, I had more hope in Doctor Moro than in him. Why, I didn't know if there even was a Doctor Moro. I had only the assurance of that fox Volpe, who had tricked me and taken all my money; yet I pinned my hopes on a man I had never seen instead of Master Giuseppe, who had given me the ability to walk and talk. But my brain was clogged with chocolate then, and I couldn't think clearly.

I also told Father about Gregorio and asked him to tell Signora Samsa what had happened to her son. The news that Gregorio was alive might quench her grief a little, even though her beloved son was now an insect. I ended the letter with a profession of love. I told Father I loved him and wanted to return as a flesh-and-blood boy who would make him proud. Those words came from the heart, and as I wrote them I thought I felt my nose shrink just a little, though when I looked in the mirror it was no shorter. I put the letter under the candle, blew it out, and returned to bed.

Gregorio woke me from a fitful sleep an hour before dawn. "It's time we were off," he chirped softly in my ear. He fed on some crumbs that had fallen to the floor while I gathered my few belongings together: a blanket, my extra shirt and pants, and the jackknife Father had given me when I began my apprenticeship. I took two hard rolls from the cupboard for breakfast and lunch, wrapping them in the blanket with my clothes. I tied the blanket roll to my back, put the knife in my pocket, and fastened Gregorio's cage to my pole. We were ready to go. I looked once around the dark, silent kitchen, then opened the door and stepped out into the night.

Chapter 11

By the time we reached Romagnano the last of the dew was gone from the grass. We made for the biggest inn in town to inquire if Volpe and Gatto had stopped there after fleecing me. The innkeeper nodded vigorously when I described the two men. They had stayed at that very inn two nights earlier.

"Very free they were with their money too," he chortled. "They ate and drank well, even bought drinks for the house. I relieved them of seven lire before they departed."

I walked out of the inn, the chocolate inside bubbling with rage and my cheeks burning with frustration. Even if I found them I wouldn't be able to recover my money! Gregorio sought to calm me down.

"Think, Pinocchio! All is not lost. Those rogues wouldn't run through all their money in a single night; they must have more."

"If we find them, Gregorio, I'll take what's due me and more, by any means possible; you can be sure of that," I vowed grimly.

"Pinocchio, what would Gabriela think of your attitude? It was just that thought that led to your great fall. You were determined to take by any means what was due you. That's what animals do, too, only they don't brood about it. I was only too willing to join you in taking your due, and I fell with you."

I had no answer for Gregorio, so we left Romagnano in silence. The day was fair, even more delightful than the day before; and little by little my foul mood dissolved. Soon we were striding along, admiring the farms and fields around us and conversing cheerfully about the road ahead.

"Pinocchio, do you think Doctor Moro really exists? I'm sure Volpe is still a fox and Gatto a cat, but I can't deny that they have been shaped into something very like men. Someone must have done that."

"I'd like to believe in Doctor Moro," I replied. "I must make myself believe in him, for without him I have no hope."

"Well, even if there is no Doctor Moro, we have a wide world before us. Maybe we'll find another way to become real boys."

We fell silent as the miles slipped by and the sun climbed higher. I was getting hot and tired, and soon my stomach was growling. When the sun reached its zenith I paused to rest just a minute under a flowering almond tree, the only shade in sight. Before I knew it I had devoured both rolls. I rose to my feet, still hungry but ready to press on to the next town, which was a long seven miles away. We would have no water till we got there, and both of us were parched.

I plodded on, too tired to respond to Gregorio's attempts to encourage me on the way. By two o'clock fatigue had wrapped itself around me like a cloak on a warm day. As the town came into sight, still a good mile away, we came upon a wall of fieldstone bordering the south side of the road. I threw myself down in its shadow to regain a little strength before trudging the last hot, dusty stretch to our goal.

As I slumped against the wall my eyes fell on a farmer on the other side of the road. The man was beating his miserable donkey in a fruitless attempt to make it pull a plow. He finally gave up flogging the beast and sat down by a large basket lying at the edge of the field, from which he began to pull out bread, cheese, and wine. If he couldn't work, he would eat.

The farmer was a filthy man. His skin was grimy, his black hair was gray with dust, and his clothes were so dirty it was impossible to tell what color they once had been. But his bread and cheese were white enough: clearly, his wife kept a clean kitchen. I grew even more famished as I watched the man eat.

"Gregorio, I am weary from hunger, and thirsty, too," I complained. "I need food and drink more than rest, but we have no food and no money. What shall we do?"

"Maybe that farmer would share some of his lunch with you," the cricket suggested. "He seems to have twice as much as he can eat." Gregorio didn't have to persuade me to try the farmer's charity. I crossed the road, smiled my biggest, broadest, friendliest smile, and introduced myself.

"Good sir, please allow me to make your acquaintance. My name is Pinocchio, son of the famous woodcarver Gepetto. I am journeying to Genoa and find that I have run out of food. Would I be presuming on your generosity if I were to beg a small morsel from the leftovers of your lunch?"

The farmer looked up and glowered. Apparently, lunch had not improved his mood. I flinched, expecting a curse or a kick in the ribs; but to my relief he replied with nothing more bruising than bitter words:

"Why, you must be kin to this donkey of mine. He thinks he can eat without working. I guess it's only man who must work for a living."

Gregorio squeaked excitedly: "Tell him you'll work for food, Pinocchio! It's the only way you'll get anything to eat." My friend's suggestion displeased me, for I was as lazy as any real boy, but I could see that it was work or go hungry.

"Signor, I would be quite willing to work for food and drink."

"Really! Well, perhaps you are human and not an animal after all. Agreed. Come to work for me. You can start now, and eat to your heart's content this evening."

"Signor, I must have food now or I'll be too weak to work," I begged.

"Oh, all right. Help yourself to half a loaf—no more, now—and that small piece of gorgonzola right there. My, you were hungry, weren't you?—wolfed it right down! You may also drink one-quarter of the water in that jug—that's enough!"

After washing the bread and cheese down with the water I followed the farmer out into the field to where the donkey stood stubbornly in front of the plow. The man unharnessed his beast, and before I knew what was happening he had yoked me to the plow instead. That wasn't what I expected at all!

"Well, what did you think I would have you do?" the farmer laughed. You don't see any other work to be done in this field, do you? We must plow before we can plant. Forward, boy!"

With those words he pulled out a whip from his side and cracked it over my head. I strained against the harness and began to move slowly down the field, the plow burying the old stubble and turning up fresh, dark earth.

"But Signor!" I cried, turning around, "Plowing is for beasts, not human beings!" He answered with a crack of the whip that stung my legs. Maddened more by fear than pain, I pushed against the yoke for all I was worth.

The day drew on and the sun dipped toward the horizon. I had done two long furrows and felt I couldn't go another yard when the farmer pulled on the reins.

With those words he pulled out a whip from his side and cracked it over my head. I strained against the harness and began to move slowly down the field….

"That's enough for today. I have to admit that you make a fine donkey. We should be finished with this field in a week. Then I may rent you out to my neighbor. His beast died this winter."

"But I am a free boy, not a beast of burden. I only agreed to work for food and water."

"Why, that's what I give all my animals. I'll certainly keep my end of the bargain. We're going back to the farmstead now, where I will feed you."

On arriving at the barnyard, I expected the farmer to unyoke me and take me into his kitchen for supper. To my surprise and horror, he led me into the barn instead. There he finally relieved me of the hated harness and shoved me into a stall, ankle-deep in mire, which he latched.

"Plenty of oats and water for you there," he said, roaring with laughter, "Just what I give all my beasts! Giacomo Lavoratore always keeps his promise! And I'm providing you with a bed and a roof over your head, too, above and beyond what we agreed on! Oh, sometimes my humanity moves me to tears!" Farmer Lavoratore laughed till the tears stained his dirty cheeks. Then he went off to the farmhouse, where his wife had supper waiting for him.

I climbed up on the manger and wiped the filth off my fouled shoes. I had no intention of eating the donkey's grain, but out of curiosity I looked in the feeding trough. The oats—what there was of them—crawled with maggots. Thin green scum floated on top of the water the poor beast had to drink. I shuddered.

"We've got to get out of here quick as we can," I whispered. "Gregorio, can you slip the latch?"

"No, I'm not nearly strong enough to do that," he replied. "But I have an idea. Let me out of my cage. Then stand away from the door."

When Gregorio was free he hopped onto the back of the donkey, which the old farmer had tied up in the passage outside the stall. Settling down in the animal's right ear, the cricket began to fidget and chirp until he drove the poor creature quite mad. The beast began to kick and lash out with its hooves, and it was not long till a chance blow shattered the stall door. Gregorio returned to me and I popped him back in his cage. The donkey soon settled down and I was able to leave the stall safely.

But before we could flee from the barn, Farmer Lavoratore burst in, a napkin still tucked under his chin and a braided leather whip coiled in one hand. "What's going on in here?" he demanded. He eyed the damage; then his gaze fell on me.

"So this is how you repay my generosity? Now you shall feel my wrath!" The wicked man snapped his whip back, meaning to lash me on the forward stroke, but a shriek behind him caused the farmer to wheel around. There were Volpe and Gatto, entangled in the whip! It seems they had crept into the barn intending to spend the night in the warm hay. When the donkey raised the commotion that brought Lavoratore running from his kitchen, they had tried to sneak out behind the farmer's back, but the backlash of the whip caught them first.

Volpe and Gatto struggled free from the coils and took off out the barn door. Lavoratore followed after in the darkness, snapping his whip and shouting. He had forgotten about me.

"Hang on, Gregorio! We're getting out of here fast," I shouted. I grabbed my blanket roll and started to run; but a gleam of gold from the dirt and straw brought me to a quick halt. A leather purse with gold ducats spilling out was lying right in front of me! I scooped up the purse and the loose coins and shoved them in my pocket, then dashed out into the night. I made for the road and didn't stop running until I reached the safety of the town.

Chapter 12

The country road became a cobbled street as it entered the town. I slowed to a fast walk and followed the street as it ran between tall, darkened buildings straight to the piazza. I stopped in the shadowy mouth of the street and looked left, right, and across the square. The silver light of a full moon reflected off the whitewashed walls and polished cobblestones, turning the piazza into a box of light. No one was to be seen.

I stepped warily into the naked moonlight and began to examine the purse I had snatched from the floor of Farmer Lavoratore's barn. It was made of soft, limp pigskin and was closed by a drawstring—a very common sort of purse. The bag bore a "V " monogram—obviously for Volpe! I counted the coins: 16 gold ducats!

"Look at that, Gregorio!" I exclaimed. "This is Volpe's purse! I've exacted more than my due, as I said. Sixteen ducats will keep us for months. I intend to spend the night in the finest inn this town affords and order their most expensive supper. We'll still have enough to meet our needs until we find the secret of becoming boys or I run down and die, whichever comes first. Let's eat, drink, and be merry."

I half-expected Gregorio to lecture me about making free with money that wasn't my own, for he had become something of a conscience to me; but that night he seemed as excited and ready to celebrate our good fortune as I was.

"There are bright lights down that street, Pinocchio," said my friend, pointing with an antenna. "They're sure to come from a trattoria." (In our part of Italy a trattoria is a kind of inn offering hearty country cooking as well as lodging.)

The lights turned out to be iron lanterns of the old fashion flanking the door of an inn bearing the name La Tavola Rossa. The inn looked substantial; the noise within told us it was well patronized. Gregorio volunteered that Carpignano (that was the name of the town) probably offered no better food and lodging, and we decided to search no further. Before drawing near to the lighted entrance I put one gold ducat in my pocket and stuffed the purse in my blanket roll. No reason to advertise how much money you are carrying! By this time I considered myself to be quite worldly-wise. I had learned from my mistakes; no one was going to fool or cheat me again.

The landlord welcomed me with a bow and a warm smile. I told him I wanted supper as well as a room, and he showed me to the commons, where other travelers were already dining. I chose a table in the corner as far removed as possible from the other guests. I didn't want them staring at us while Gregorio and I talked.

"Tonight we offer roast pork and also tortellini. Which would the young gentleman prefer?" asked the innkeeper.

"Both," I replied, "I am very hungry. And a glass of your best wine, if you please."

"Roast pork *and* tortellini? Very good, Signor," stuttered the landlord, surprised at my appetite. He wouldn't have been at all surprised if he had known all I had gone through that day.

Before long our host returned with a glass of Chianti, both hot dishes, and a large loaf of crusty bread. After he had set the food and wine before us he retired to the kitchen and we were left alone. We fell at once to eating and didn't speak a single a word to each other until I had finished all the pork, half the tortellini, and the Chianti, which was quite superior. Gregorio sampled a little of everything but preferred the bread.

"I can hardly believe the change in our fortunes, Gregorio! Two hours ago we were locked up like beasts of burden; now we dine like the rich! God has rewarded me for my suffering."

"Is that what Barbe Filippo would say?"

"Well, I suppose Barbe would look at what happened today differently. He would say that God has been merciful and gracious to me without my deserving it at all."

"But you think you do deserve it because of what you suffered at the hands of Volpe and Gatto."

"Yes, I do. I'm really a nice person—well, a nice puppet—don't you think? I deserve the good things of this life. I deserve to live, Gregorio. God owes it to me to turn me into a real boy."

"Pinocchio, we both want desperately to be turned into real boys, but neither of us can honestly say we deserve it. Think about the bad things you've done in your short lifetime. You disobeyed in the matter of the cake; you played pranks at school; you picked Signora Fiore's flowers."

"You're a fine one to point out my errors, you spineless creature," I retorted. "Your whole boyhood was one of deviltry before you fell along with me."

"Don't I know it!" Gregorio squeaked ruefully. "I'm sorry for that now. Being sorry doesn't make it better, but I think that somehow we need to be truly sorry before anything better can happen."

"I can justify every one of the so-called bad things you're throwing up to me, Gregorio. I suppose you think that if Volpe and Gatto were to walk in that door right now I ought to give back all but seven coppers."

"I *should* say that, Pinocchio, but I admit that I too would find it hard to return the money. Sometimes it's hard to do the right thing, sometimes it's too hard. But the hard thing would be the right thing; you must admit that."

I was feeling too drowsy after the wine and the meal to argue with my friend. Besides, in my excitement I had gotten a little loud and some of the other guests were looking at me curiously. No doubt they thought I was arguing with myself.

Lowering my voice, I brought our conversation to an end: "We can continue this discussion on the road tomorrow if you like, but it's getting too deep for me tonight. Let's find our room and get some sleep now."

Gregorio agreed. I put him back in his cage, grabbed my blanket roll, and went upstairs to find my room. It was clean and warm, with a window overlooking the piazza. I bolted the door, drew the curtains closed, and let Gregorio out of his cage (he had expressed a desire to sleep on the hearth). I had forgotten how exhausted I was until I looked at the bed; then fatigue overcame me all at once. I slipped under the covers and slept dreamlessly till morning.

When I awoke the sun was already shining strongly through the window. As I lay under the warm comforter, I could see the sky. It was pure azure, without a cloud in sight. A soft breeze came through the open window.

Open window! I jumped to my feet, my heart beating rapidly. I had closed the window and drawn the curtains before going to bed!

"Gregorio! Somebody broke into our room last night!" I hurried to the table where I had laid out my clothes. The purse lay next to my shirt, just where I had left it. I counted the coins. All fifteen ducats were there. I sighed with relief and my heart slowed down.

"I can hardly believe the change in our fortunes, Gregorio! Two hours ago we were locked up like beasts of burden; now we dine like the rich! God has rewarded me for my suffering."

"Our burglar must have been blind; or perhaps something frightened him before he could finish the job," I called to Gregorio. "Volpe's purse was in plain sight but the intruder didn't take it. Not a single coin is missing." I looked at the table again. Everything was there: my trousers, shirt, bedroll, jackknife, Volpe's purse—everything but Gregorio's cage.

"Gregorio, the foolish man took your cage! What could he want it for?" My question was met with silence. An awful thought came to me. I rushed to the hearth and got down on my hands and knees.

"Gregorio, answer me! Let me know you're here." No answer. I searched every corner of the room, calling out my friend's name, more sure with every passing minute that I wouldn't find him. After an hour I stopped looking and sat down on the edge of the bed. I wept. Gregorio had been kidnapped!

I pulled myself together and tried to think. No doubt one of those curious guests in the commons had seen enough to realize that I wasn't arguing with myself but with Gregorio. A talking cricket would fetch a high price from any carnival. The thief had probably sold him already. I would have to track down my friend and rescue him.

I went over to the window and looked down. No burglar could scale that wall. He must have had a ladder; and that meant he lived in town or had a townsman for a friend, for travelers don't pack ladders around with them. I went downstairs to talk with my host.

A maid was wiping down the tables in the commons but the landlord was not to be found there or in the kitchen. She told me her master had gone to the bakery for the day's bread. He would return in about a quarter hour by way of the alley behind the inn. I stepped out the kitchen door to catch him before he entered the inn. I wanted to make my inquiries privately.

There it was, leaning against the wall by the kitchen door: a ladder, surely *the* ladder. I went back inside the inn and found the maid mopping the taproom floor.

"Signorina," I began innocently, "Is there much crime in Carpignano?"

"As much as in any town nowadays, I imagine," she replied. "The times are very bad."

"I supposed as much," I answered. "That's why I was so surprised to see your master's ladder leaning against the wall out back, where any thief could carry it off in the night."

The maid laid down her mop and smiled at me. "Oh really? He always keeps it locked up in the storeroom when it's not in use; he must have put it outside this very morning. No doubt he will want me to wash the upper story windows today, though it was but two weeks ago I washed them last."

The maid went on to tell me everything she had done around the inn for the last month. I was glad she was a talker, for it was clear to me that her master was in on the burglary and that I would get no help from him.

"Well, you certainly keep this house shiny and spotless. The beds are soft too, at least mine was, and supper last night was excellent. I imagine this inn is a popular spot for townsfolk to meet as well as a favorite stop for travelers."

"Oh, yes," she replied, "Many of our own people dine here. Why, Signor Ladrone, the master's closest friend, was in the commons last night when you came. He stayed till after I put out the light, talking with the master in the kitchen till I don't know when."

"Ladrone! My father's best comrade in the army was named Ladrone," I lied. "What would his Christian name be?"

"Carlo. Carlo Ladrone is his name."

"The very one! Listen, could you tell me where his house is? I'd like to look him up and talk with him."

"I could direct you to his very door, but it would do you no good today. Signor Ladrone owns a small carnival; he's gone for months at a time. He was home for a short visit but he left this morning. Master had me pack a lunch for him just two hours ago."

"I am going to Genoa," I said. "If he is going that way, I may meet him on the road."

"Well, you're out of luck. He turned right when he crossed the piazza; that means he's going west on the Torino road."

I made more small talk with the maid; then I ordered breakfast. I was anxious to get on the road, but if I didn't make a fuss about the theft of my cricket the landlord would get suspicious.

He arrived just when the maid set breakfast before me. I told him about the theft of my "pet," as I phrased it, allowing him to think I was trying to conceal Gregorio's ability to talk. The old hypocrite expressed shock and sympathy, and insisted on refunding the price of my food and lodging.

"This is such an embarrassment for me," the innkeeper moaned. "It must have been that red-haired man with the curly beard who was eating in the commons last night. He looked suspicious even then; but he paid, so what could I do? I know for a fact that he took the road south to Genoa. You can catch him if you hurry."

I knew perfectly well there had been no red-haired man in the commons the previous night, but I thanked that lying innkeeper for the information with as much pretended sincerity as I could work up.

I left town by the Genoa road, but once out of sight of curious eyes I cut across fields till I struck the Torino road. It was the first of May. I had only six months till I ran down; but I was determined to spend them all searching for Gregorio if it came to that.

Chapter 13

I had no idea where to begin my search. The broad plain of the Po is thickly settled with villages and towns; roads crisscross in all directions. Probably a dozen small carnivals roam from town to town during the warm months, going wherever the owner fancies. Ladrone's carnival could have been anywhere. I didn't even know what Ladrone looked like: with chocolate seething inside I had forgotten to ask the maid to describe him. My chances of coming upon the thief were nil.

Then I thought to pray.

"Signor, God of my father Gepetto: I am not a real boy; I have not been baptized; and I do not know if you will hear my prayer. I admit that I have not been a very good puppet. Gregorio has not been very good either. But you are loving and forgiving. Please help me to rescue my friend. If you do, I promise I will be good and obey all your commandments all the time. Amen."

I didn't feel comfortable praying like that. I knew I was supposed to think of myself as a sinner, but I could think of many worse than me—that wicked innkeeper, for one. And I wasn't sure I could be as good as I promised to be. But it seemed to me I had to give God something in return for the favor I was asking. I prayed out of despair, not faith; surely God knew that. How would he lead me to Gregorio? What would he do to help me rescue my friend when I finally tracked Ladrone down? I didn't believe in miracles; and even if I had, I couldn't see why God would want to help me even if he could. Still, I was at the end of my rope, and prayed fervently and often as I trudged along the road to Torino.

I asked each traveler I met if he had seen a man with a cricket in a cage. Some looked at me as if I were crazy; some ignored me and hurried by as though I were not there. Others were pleasant enough and talked freely, but no one had seen the man I sought. I concluded that Ladrone was keeping his prize hidden from view as he made his way back to his carnival.

Every seven or eight miles I came on a village or town. In each one I rounded up a half-dozen street urchins and loosened their tongues with a lira or two. My sharp-eyed informants were able to paint detailed pictures of all the strangers that had passed their way that day, but none remembered a man with a cricket in a cage.

The weather turned hot and sticky. Noon found me in open country, discouraged and hungry. I stopped a farmer on his way to market and bought some dried figs. A wall as tall as a man ran between the road and a vineyard on my right. I decided to climb over the wall to eat and rest a bit in its shade. I shoved the figs in my pocket, backed up three steps, and made a run at the wall. I jumped, caught hold of the top, and vaulted over. On the way down—when it was too late to do anything—I saw two vagabonds sleeping peacefully below me. I didn't even have time to cry out before I landed squarely on them. The sleepers awoke with a painful gasp and turned their shocked faces towards me: Volpe and Gatto again!

Those two scoundrels were a pitiful sight. They were covered with red welts and purple bruises—Farmer Lavoratore had got some good licks in before they escaped. I hadn't done them any good either, landing on them like that. Still, Volpe managed a weak smile and spoke when he recovered his breath.

"Why look, Signor Gatto, it is young Master Pinocchio again! We are glad to have been of service to him, diverting the wrath of that wicked farmer, are we not?"

"Yes; so glad to have been of service to you, young Master," wheezed Gatto.

I was in no mood to tolerate their oily pleasantries. I had to find Gregorio before the trail grew completely cold.

"Listen to me, you scabby vermin. You used flattery and guile to swindle me out of my seven lire in the Field of Wishes, but I'm not going to be taken in by you again. I happen to know you are penniless now. It so happens that I've come into some money; but I've also lost my pet cricket. Do you remember it?"

"Yes; you carried it in a cage behind your back," replied the fox. "Such a shame that your pet is missing, is it not, Signor Gatto?"

"A terrible shame, to be sure," murmured the cat.

With half-closed eyes Volpe casually asked, "Why do you tell us this if you are displeased with your faithful friends?"

"My cricket was stolen. I'm willing to pay for information that will lead me to the thief. I know him only by the name Ladrone. Gregorio, my cricket, is trained and can do surprising tricks.

Ladrone owns a carnival; I'm sure he intends to put my pet on display. I'm willing to pay money, even to rogues like you, if you can find the thief for me." I took Volpe's purse out of my pocket and jingled it before his swollen face. Volpe's bloodshot eyes bulged; Gatto hissed.

"Don't think about trying to take this away from me, you flea-ridden creatures. I was more than a match for you before you were reduced to hobbling about as you do now. God has punished you for your wickedness and repaid me for the loss I suffered at your hands." I enjoyed giving those villains a tongue-lashing; the chocolate within me percolated nicely as I warmed to the task. Then I thought of Gregorio, and the pleasure of venting my feelings melted away. I fell silent.

Seeing that I had paused in my outburst, Volpe spoke up. "Master, we confess that we sinned against you and violated the trust you placed in us. Allow us to win back your confidence and favor. We did see a man carrying your cricket. At the time we thought you had sold it, being in desperate straits. We would be pleased to lead you to that man."

"Where is my friend, that is, my pet?" I cried.

"Young Master Pinocchio is hasty," the fox replied. "First we must come to an agreement regarding the expenses Signor Gatto and I have borne in obtaining this information. Surely a young man of high character like yourself would want to repay us for the pains we suffered locating the thief. We will accept only a token payment, of course, and that only to maintain your reputation as a gentleman of honor who takes care of his friends. I should say that sixteen ducats would be a small amount to preserve the reputation of your personage."

Anger flared up in my wooden heart as Volpe stated his terms. I wanted to slap that bland, smiling face, but I stifled my feelings. The fox had the information I needed and he knew it.

With effort I smiled back at him and replied: "How could I hold a grudge? What you propose is certainly fair; but I no longer have sixteen ducats. Here, see for yourselves." With those words I turned the purse upside down and shook it, taking care to hold back several coins while I let the rest tumble into my left hand. Nine shining ducats fell out; four were concealed in the folds of the bag grasped in my right hand. While Volpe and Gatto devoured the coins with greedy eyes, I shoved the bag with the remaining ducats into my pocket where they would not clink and betray my trickery.

"I will give you two ducats now as a gesture of goodwill. The other seven are yours when I lay eyes on Ladrone and Gregorio. Agreed?"

The fox wanted to bargain. "Surely it would show more goodwill to give us seven now and two when we have brought you to your cricket's captor, don't you think?"

"Frankly, I don't have that much goodwill left for two misbegotten creatures like you. But I will agree to give you four ducats now, five when you have brought me to the man."

Volpe was persistent. "Master, one must go the extra mile, as the Savior says. Let us say five now, four later." Gatto chimed right in: "Five now, four later."

It was time to wrap up the haggling. "Very well, five now," I said, and counted out five ducats to Volpe. I insisted that we start off without delay. Volpe and Gatto readily agreed: the rest of the money weighed on their minds.

"We must turn around and head back towards Carpignano," Volpe said. "We saw the man you seek in San Vittorio, which is not on the main road; that would be why you missed him. You passed the turn for San Vittorio three miles back, though you probably took no notice of it; it is an unimportant place."

Volpe and Gatto were still suffering from their beating the night before, and our progress was slow. Still, we reached the crossroads in less than two hours. San Vittorio was less than a mile from there. We arrived at the piazza at three o'clock, just as the church bell was tolling *nones*. We found the piazza crowded with all kinds of people: children, mothers with babies, and old men; wayfarers, townsmen, and peasants. The reason became obvious as we pushed through the crowd: a carnival had set up on the south side of the square.

"Young Master Pinocchio, the man you seek is somewhere in that throng. When we've found him we'll return and lead you to him." With those words Volpe and Gatto disappeared into the crush of carnivalgoers.

I had no choice but to wait at the edge of the crowd. I didn't have to wait long. Back the two rogues came, smiling in triumph. "Follow us." I hurried along behind them. The pair led me to a large carnival wagon standing off by itself.

"The man you seek is at this very moment inside that wagon with your cricket." I crept up to the door, which was slightly ajar, and peeked inside. A powerfully built man with a walrus mustache and bushy eyebrows sat at a tiny table. He was asleep, his head resting on the table, his mustache quivering as he snored softly. The sharp smell of sour wine filled the wagon. On the table next to his head rested an empty bottle and Gregorio's cage. The wagon was too dark to see clearly, but I thought I could make out the dark form of a cricket on the bottom of the cage. I was ready to creep in and rescue him right then when I felt a tug on my shirt. I turned around and found Volpe and Gatto.

"We've kept our end of the bargain, young sir," the fox whispered. "If it's not too much trouble, could you give us the remaining four ducats now, before you attempt to remove your pet by stealth? We would like to be gone in case Signor Ladrone should awaken, and trouble follow."

I silently counted the money into Volpe's outstretched paw. He took it and the two rogues disappeared without a word before I could hiss "Good riddance!"

I turned back to the wagon and peered inside again. All was as it had been a minute earlier, Ladrone snoring and at peace with the world. I opened the door just far enough to slip inside, taking care not to let the sun fall on the man's face. I stepped up into the wagon and tiptoed towards the table. Gregorio saw me, but I held my finger to my lips; he quivered with joy but made no sound. So far, so good.

I removed the cage from the table and turned to go. Without warning, before I could take a single step towards the door the sleeping man shot out a hand and gripped my neck like a varmint trap snares a weasel. I was well caught, and knew it.

"Master Pinocchio, I've been expecting you!" the wicked man laughed. "Your friends were kind enough to inform me just a few minutes ago that you would come calling shortly. I've been providing hospitality to your cricket. Please allow me to be your host too."

With that, Ladrone clapped me in a large cage, such as might be used to contain a lynx or wolf. He put Gregorio's cage inside mine; then he went out, closing the wagon door and leaving us alone.

With that, Ladrone clapped me in a large cage, such as might be used to contain a lynx or wolf. He put Gregorio's cage inside mine; then he went out, closing the wagon door and leaving us alone.

Chapter 14

As soon as we were alone Gregorio began to talk excitedly. "Pinocchio! Until Volpe and Gatto appeared minutes ago I thought I'd never see you again. I was overjoyed when they told Ladrone you were coming; I knew you would ransom me. I never thought Ladrone would make you a captive too."

"And I never dreamed Volpe and Gatto would betray me. We're both too innocent to be abroad in this wicked world; or maybe we're just too clever for our own good."

Our conversation was cut off by Ladrone's return. He carried a loaf of bread and a small wedge of Parmesan cheese.

"I've brought you something to eat, Pinocchio. I believe in caring for my investments, and that's what you and your cricket are, investments."

I was hungry and started to eat at once. Between mouthfuls I cautiously began to feel out Ladrone's intentions.

"Naturally, sir, I'm unhappy about being in this cage, but I sense it would be useless to ask you to release us at this time. Perhaps you would be good enough to tell me why I am your prisoner—or your investment, as you put it."

"I'm more than willing to tell you why you're my guest—that's a better term than either prisoner or investment, don't you think? It's important that you know why I intend to provide you with such hospitality. It's really to the benefit of us all, you know. This world is full of wicked, vicious men who would do bad things to you and the cricket. I offer you protection. In return, you have only to appear on my stage, entertaining the good country people of the towns we pass through."

"The work is easy," he continued. "You and the cricket have only to talk, that's all. You will make me the greatest ventriloquist in the whole world. The secret is that you really will talk, but the people won't know that. You and I will open the show. I'll ask you questions and you'll answer me. My lips will never move. Then I'll eat and drink while you, my wooden dummy, keep on talking. For my finale I'll allow the spectators to gag me while the cricket talks. You don't sing, do you? It would be splendid if you could sing also."

"It's very kind of you to extend such an opportunity to us," I replied, "but we have a quest, a matter of life and death, that we must pursue without delay. I'm afraid we have to decline to appear in your show, though we're greatly honored that you should ask."

Ladrone smiled as a wolf smiles when contemplating a tender lamb. "Let me make you an offer you can't refuse, woodenhead. You'll appear on stage with me and you'll make me look very, very good, or I'll squash your friend with my boot and throw you into the stove this very minute."

"It seems we have no choice," I said. "But I won't sing."

"Good! I'm glad you're being sensible about this. You'll find that I'm not an unreasonable master. I won't insist on your singing. Here, have some more cheese."

I took the cheese and gave a few crumbs to Gregorio, wrapping the rest in my handkerchief. I was still hungry, but I was too excited to eat, for a plan was forming in my mind. Later that afternoon, when Ladrone went out again, I told Gregorio my idea. He agreed that it was probably our only hope of escaping from Ladrone's grasp; but we would have to wait for the right time.

The right time didn't present itself immediately. Every morning and afternoon we put on a show. Ladrone's wagon had a stage built on the front end. The facade was covered with dingy gilded plaster cherubs and grapevines that clearly had not been molded by Michelangelo. Over the curtain stretched a canvas banner proclaiming in faded crimson script that Carlo Ladrone was the world's greatest ventriloquist. At ten o'clock and again at four our captor would struggle into a threadbare dinner jacket that had once been white but had never been large enough for his powerful chest and arms. Then he would go out on stage and call at the top of his lungs, announcing that the greatest ventriloquist in the world would demonstrate his amazing ability on that very stage in five minutes. Just one lira would admit the spectator to the area in front of the stage.

In fifteen minutes or so, when Ladrone had gathered as many curious folk as he could persuade to part with a lira, the show would begin. Our captor would sit on a chair with me on his knee. To the crowd it appeared that his hand rested on my shoulder in fatherly fashion; actually, he held me in an iron grip. To make doubly sure I wouldn't give him the slip and run away, Ladrone had tethered

Gregorio to his own watch chain. The clever rogue knew I wouldn't forsake my friend even if I could free myself from his grasp.

The show itself was a great success with the people. Ladrone would talk pleasantly to me, and I would answer him with pert retorts while his face remained as motionless as a marble bust. Then he would drink coffee, eat spaghetti, or whistle while I launched into a soliloquy. Gregorio was an even bigger hit. The spectators were amazed that a *basso profundo* like Ladrone could squeak out words three octaves above his range when Gregorio was talking.

Our chance finally came nine days later. Two carabinieri, regional police officers, stopped to watch the show. I waited until Ladrone was drinking a glass of water. Then I shouted out words he didn't expect.

"Look, Boss, those are the ugliest carabinieri I've ever seen. I'll bet the fat one can't even mount a horse anymore. They get that way by eating rich food at the tables of the wealthy."

Ladrone spluttered, spraying water over the table. Before he could speak, Gregorio chirped right up: "The tall one looks like a horse thief—or maybe just a horse. Do you suppose he's going to ask the Boss for a bribe to keep the carnival open, like he did last week?"

"Why not?" I asked, "The fat one always gets his share; his comrade must be just as greedy. It's time the people rose up and put an end to it. All power to the people! Down with the corrupt police!"

That was too much for the carabinieri. They seized Ladrone and began to drag him away.

"No, no; you're making a big mistake!" he protested, terrified. "I didn't say those things; the dummy and the cricket did it on their own. They can really talk, you know. Here, take them and question them. You'll see; you can make them talk." Ladrone thrust Gregorio into the hands of the fat officer and shoved me at his thin companion, who let me fall in a heap on the stage. Gregorio chirped like an ordinary cricket; I lay silently where I fell.

The carabinieri ignored us and snarled at our captor: "First you insult us with words and now you insult our intelligence. You're coming with us." With rough hands and much more force than necessary, the carabinieri put manacles on Ladrone and dragged him away, still babbling denials. The crowd followed them, hoping to see a good beating. We were left alone.

They seized Ladrone and began to drag him away.
"No, no; you're making a big mistake!" he protested, terrified. "I didn't say those things; the dummy and the cricket did it on their own.

I picked up Gregorio and retired inside the wagon. There I removed the chain from my friend's neck and put him in his cage again. I collected my own belongings as well as enough food for several decent meals.

"Let's get out of here and back on the road," I said. "I won't feel safe till we're far away from this town. We have no time to waste."

We left San Vittorio unnoticed.

Chapter 15

Five roads came together at San Vittorio. We left the village on the one winding away to the southeast, hoping to hit on the great Genoa road in a day or two. My friend was very talkative, and our conversation turned to the ways of God.

"I don't know much about God, Pinocchio. My parents seldom went to church. Even when we did, we heard very little preaching. But Gepetto took you to church every Sunday; and I understand Barbe Filippo preaches for an hour straight. You must have learned a good deal about God. Tell me: Do you think God sent Volpe and Gatto, wicked traitors that they were, to lead you to me?"

"Well, I prayed that he would allow me to rescue you, and in an hour Volpe and Gatto were leading me straight to San Vittorio. I never would have thought to go there on my own. I have to think that God sent those rogues to guide me to you. Even though they betrayed me, we found a way to escape. Yes, I think it all was the Lord's doing."

Gregorio scratched his head with a hind leg. "I find it hard to understand why the Lord would use evil men—or whatever Volpe and Gatto really are—to bring good to pass. How can he use bad means if he is good?"

"I have no idea; remember, my brain is full of chocolate. But it seems that he does use the wicked to do good. And that gives me hope he will lead us to some means of becoming real boys no matter what troubles we may go through. We've certainly had our share of troubles so far."

In talking about the Lord, I remembered my promise to keep all His commandments. I felt very grateful to God then and silently renewed my vow to be good. It wouldn't be long, however, before I forgot it entirely, as you shall see.

Gregorio kept up his chatter. "It's a good thing Gepetto doesn't know all the trouble you've gotten into. I'm sure he's worried about you as it is. What can he do, after all, but wait for your return?"

We would find out much later that Father was not waiting for my return. He had not even finished reading the note I left when he decided to leave the village at once to look for me.

Chapter 15

Father had made a shrewd guess that I would head for Genoa. All the boys in our village vowed to leave home and seek their fortunes when they were old enough, though hardly anyone ever did, and they all thought that Genoa and Rome were the places to go if you wanted to make your fortune. Genoa was much closer than Rome, and Father resolved to look for me there first. If he couldn't find me in Genoa, he would continue on to Rome.

Before leaving the village Father went to see Giuseppe. He showed his friend my note and asked him to look after the shop while he was away.

"It will be a comfort knowing that you are there carving toys for the children while I am searching for my son," Father said.

"We'll do more than that, dear friend," Giuseppe replied. "I told you that my plan to turn Pinocchio into a real boy was almost ready, but I didn't tell you the plan itself. Now I will tell you the reason.

"The plan is not really mine; it is my son's plan. Giovanni told me he couldn't put his plan into effect until the time was right. That's why you had to wait. Well, my son says that the time is now at hand. Oh, if only Pinocchio had had the faith to wait one more day!"

"And now it's too late!" cried Father. "If I can't find Pinocchio in six months he'll run down and all will be lost! My chances of finding him in time are so small!"

"Don't despair, Gepetto! I told you we could do more than watch your shop. Giovanni told me that he personally will go in search of Pinocchio. He will leave Monday. Wait until Monday, Gepetto, and go with him."

"I can't bear to wait even a few days, Giuseppe. I'm worried sick about Pinocchio. I must leave today. If I find Pinocchio, I'll send for Giovanni. If Giovanni finds him first, let him send for me."

Giuseppe tried to persuade Father to wait until Giovanni could accompany him, but Father was determined to leave that very day. He did agree to write Giuseppe every week.

So by the time we had escaped from Ladrone's clutches, both Father and Giovanni were on the road looking for me. If I had known, I would have worried about Father. He wasn't a vigorous, clever young man who had learned to take care of himself in this wicked world, such as I thought myself to be. As for Giovanni, I

Giuseppe tried to persuade Father to wait until Giovanni could accompany him, but Father was determined to leave that very day. He did agree to write Giuseppe every week.

hardly knew him. If you had told me that he, not Giuseppe, had concocted the plan to change me into a real boy, I would have been even more determined to find the mysterious Doctor Moro.

We reached the Genoa highway in two days. The road was full of travelers, which was comforting to me. If we met up with any more wicked characters on our journey I could cry for help and know that many would hear my cries.

The country was dotted with inns, both in the many villages and towns we passed through and at nearly every crossroad. I had money, so we didn't have to take our chances sleeping in open fields or begging from stingy farmers. I was careful not to talk to Gregorio when others were near so that no thieving soul like Ladrone would be tempted to steal my friend.

I hadn't forgotten my promise to be good and obey all the Lord's commandments; in fact, I was looking for a chance to show Him how good I was. My chance came in a town called Vercelli. As we were passing through the piazza, a beggar asked us for alms. He was a pitiful sight. The unfortunate man was both blind and lame. He sat cross-legged with a cane lying on the cobblestones beside him, hands outstretched in supplication. His matted gray hair and ragged clothing cried out as painfully as his cracked broken voice. It was market day, and the piazza was filled with people, but all turned their eyes away and hurried past him. No one would give him a single lira.

I, too, was about to pass by when I remembered my vow. I stopped in front of the wretch and smiled my most compassionate smile. He was blind, so of course he could not see me, but the people in the crowd could. I unhurriedly undid the strings of my purse and pulled out a ten-lire note, which I pressed into his hand in full view of all.

"Here is a ten-lire note for you, my good man," I said quite loudly. "May God richly bless you." I felt the chocolate bubble inside while I performed this public act of charity. I thought that strange, for it had only bubbled like that before when I was angry or greedy or in the grip of some other sin. I didn't realize how much my good deed fed my pride; I felt instead that the Lord must be very pleased with me for being so generous with my money. You will remember where I got that money in the first place, but that thought did not occur to me.

Before continuing on my way I looked around the crowd to see who had observed my act of charity. I saw a plump little girl with shining black eyes standing with a very fat, distinguished-looking gentleman at the front of the crowd. I smiled at them like a priest who had just blessed his congregation. The girl whispered something in his ear. He nodded to her. She approached me with a smile and introduced herself.

"Young man, permit me to introduce us. My name is Dido Avaro, and this gentleman is my father, Giulio Avaro. We observed your generosity to that miserable beggar and wish to commend you for your act, even though he didn't deserve it. It was a noble thing to do and reveals a noble soul. We would like to reward your good deed. Would you honor us with your presence at our dinner table this afternoon?"

Flushed with self-righteousness, I replied that I would be most pleased to accept their hospitality. As I followed them through the streets of Vercelli, I commented on the turn of events to my friend.

"Finally, Gregorio, we have fallen in with people of quality. There are true ladies and gentlemen in this world, good Christian people who recognize and reward good deeds, just like the Lord. We're in for a delightful afternoon with this charming young lady and her father."

"I hope it's the intention rather than the good done by the deed that counts with the Lord," replied Gregorio. "The young signorina was right about the beggar not deserving your alms: while you were looking around at the crowd I saw him glance at the bill you gave him to see if it really was a ten-lire note; then he jumped up and clicked his heels with delight. If he's blind and lame, so are Gatto and Volpe. The little signorina probably knew he was a fraud, but once it was too late to warn you she kindly spared your feelings and didn't tell you. As you said, she and her father seem to be true gentlefolk, people of quality."

How little Gregorio and I knew about people of quality.

Chapter 16

The Avaro estate lay a short mile south of Vercelli. A line of poplar trees ran completely around the estate just inside the wall, shielding those within from prying eyes. Signor Avaro rang a bell at the gate, and soon a servant opened it to us. A curving gravel path led towards the center of the estate. My wooden eyes bulged out as the villa came into view: it was the finest, richest house I had ever seen in my short life. We climbed a marble staircase to the main entrance and a butler opened the door—Signor Avaro didn't even have to knock!

I was shown into a high, dim hall. As my eyes grew used to the shadows I saw that the walls were covered with large portraits in heavy gilded frames. Eight generations of Avaros stared down at me as I followed my host and his daughter down a deep crimson carpet not quite as thick as the grass in the meadow. A square of bright sunlight showed through tall glass doors at the end of the hall. We passed through these into a cheerful courtyard filled with ferns and flowers. A fountain in the center of all the greenery tinkled pleasantly.

"We will dine *al fresco* this afternoon, Alberto," Signor Avaro told the butler. "Set a place for this young gentleman next to my daughter."

We sat in the shade of the cloister and talked while Alberto went about his work.

"Young man, I'm afraid I don't even know your name."

"My given name is Pinocchio, sir."

"And your family name?"

"To be honest, sir, I have no family name. I am from a small village where everyone knows everyone else simply by their Christian names. Indeed, our village itself has no name."

Dido giggled at this but her father reproved her gently. "Don't laugh, Dido. Rome began to decline when the Caesars started adding one name to another. Honest country folk with one name are much to be preferred to aristocrats with many names and airs."

"You are right, Father," the little signorina replied. "Pinocchio is handsome and good, and that is enough." She looked at me with those shining eyes. I began to feel a bit uncomfortable.

My wooden eyes bulged out as the villa came into view: it was the finest, richest house I had ever seen in my short life.

Alberto returned to announce that dinner was served. The three of us sat down at a table next to the fountain and the butler began to serve us, one course at a time. First a large plate of antipasto, enough for a dozen diners, which we devoured entirely. The antipasto was followed by the soup, a minestrone; then Alberto served the fish, bream poached in white wine, butter, and lemon sauce. I was already full when Alberto cleared away the remains of the fish; then he returned with several pasta dishes. Scarcely had I managed to sample them all when he served the main dish, chicken cacciatore swimming in rich, red sauce.

A serving maid assisted Alberto as he served the three of us. She kept my glass full: a white wine with the fish, a dark red with the pasta and chicken. As usual, I was unconcerned about the dangers of wine even though I knew that the Lord and my father would not approve of boys drinking wine.

Throughout dinner we kept up a steady conversation. In fact, I did almost all the talking. I entertained my host and little hostess with tales of life in the village, describing our colorful characters and recounting my most outlandish pranks. I didn't tell them I was a wooden boy. Strangely, they didn't seem to notice. Naturally, since I didn't tell them I was wooden I didn't tell them of my quest; I simply said that I was going to Genoa to see the sights and meet an important doctor there. I did show them Gregorio, whom I described as my pet. Dido was delighted with Gregorio, who obliged by doing some tricks.

My belly was so stuffed that it hurt to touch it, my head throbbed like a heavy cart rumbling over the bridge at Trevino, and I was wilting in the midsummer sun when Alberto finally set a bowl of chilled fruit on the table for dessert. The maid began to fill my glass with a dark, oily vermouth to wash down the fruit. I weakly waved her away.

"We always eat a light midday meal in the summer," said Signor Avaro, cleaning his teeth with an ivory toothpick. "I hope it was satisfactory."

"Oh yes," I replied. "You have been a wonderful host."

"Let me show you the villa," Signor Avaro volunteered. I would have preferred to find a place where I could sleep till my discomfort melted away but I gamely replied that nothing would give me greater pleasure than to see his ancestral home.

It seemed to me that we walked for two hours through Signor Avaro's estate. Up and down staircases without number, through cloisters and garden paths and fancy stone passageways beneath the villa—we went on till the sun began to dip low in the west.

"I thank you again for your hospitality," I said, "but now I must continue on my journey. It has been a very pleasant day."

"Oh, it's getting late. You must stay here overnight. We have plenty of guest rooms, as you have seen. Besides, there are brigands on the roads around here at night. I insist on your being our guest tonight, for your own safety and also to keep us company. You cannot imagine how lonely it is here for us, especially for Dido. She has no friends of her own age in the town."

"Surely there are many young girls Dido's age in a town as big as Vercelli."

"Of course there are other young girls, but not persons of quality. I do not allow Dido to associate with riff-raff."

It really was too late to leave Vercelli and reach another town, and Signor Avaro's warning about bandits on the road alarmed me.

"I gratefully accept your invitation to be your house guest this evening," I said.

"Excellent! Why don't you and Dido sit here and talk while I see Alberto about making up a room for you."

With that Signor Avaro left me alone with Dido in the herb garden. I was sitting on a stone bench. Dido immediately came and sat down next to me.

"Do you like it here?" she asked.

"It is very pleasant," I replied uneasily.

"Pinocchio, why don't you stay here with us? Genoa is not nearly as nice a place as Vercelli. I know; I went to Genoa once. And your important doctor can't be nicer than we are, can he? Stay here, Pinocchio! Father would put you on his payroll—you could tell your stories and make us happy. And when I'm old enough, we could marry. Dearest Pinocchio, I fell in love with you at first sight when I saw you in the piazza. I couldn't bear to have you leave!"

As Dido looked at me with a hopeful smile and her ever-shining eyes my heart sank. So that was it. I felt nothing for Dido; my heart belonged to Gabriela. How could I tell Dido this without hurting her feelings? I decided to tell her that I was a wooden boy; that should quench any love she felt for me.

"Dido, I haven't been entirely honest. I haven't told you the whole story of my life. The truth is that I am a wooden puppet, not a flesh-and-blood boy. I will never grow up. In fact, the spring inside that keeps me going will wind down in six months. Then I will die. I'm going to Genoa to find a doctor who, so I have been told, can turn me into a real boy. You see, don't you, why I can't stay?"

Dido kept smiling. Her eyes shone even more brightly as she blinked back tears.

"Oh, Pinocchio! How tragic and sad! But that's all the more reason to end your brief life here. No doctor in Genoa or anywhere else can turn you into a real boy. Stay here and let us love you until you collapse lifeless in my arms. Then you shall be my sleeping Prince Charming, and I shall carry you around and cherish your memory as long as I live, or at least until I find another boy to love. Only you'll never know about that, so you won't be hurt. Father taught me never to hurt another's feelings."

This was not the reaction I hoped for. Still, I could see that Dido wouldn't be grief-stricken at my refusal to stay.

"I'll always value your love, Dido," I replied with as sincere a face as I could put on, "but I must press on with my quest. Be very sure that if I succeed I will return to you." My nose grew a full half-inch with that lie but Dido didn't seem to notice.

At that point Signor Avaro reappeared and I turned to him. "Please excuse me from joining you at supper tonight. I got up very early and came many miles to Vercelli before you kindly took me in, and I am quite tired. I have to get an early start in the morning and would like to retire early."

"Of course; how thoughtless of us not to realize that you must be tired," my host replied. "I'll tell Alberto to lay out a tray of sandwiches by your bedroom door in case you wake up hungry in the night."

Signor Avaro called for Alberto, who appeared as if by magic. After receiving his instructions Alberto led me to my room. He left and I closed the door. Gregorio and I were finally alone.

"What kind of family is this, Gregorio?" I asked. "They seem refined, but they eat like gluttons. And Dido! She thinks she loves me, but she would have me stay here even if it means my death."

Gregorio responded thoughtfully. "Their refinement is all on the outside, Pinocchio. It's only a matter of manners and taste. You attracted their attention with an act of charity befitting a person of quality. They invited you here to show you that they are also people of quality. Their home, their servants, and their food shout out, 'We are people of quality.'

"But inside, Pinocchio, they are no better than Volpe or Gatto, or Lavoratore or Ladrone, or you or me. Signor and Signorina Avaro deny themselves nothing. The only difference between them and us is that they can have whatever they want. No wonder they're nice. Let them be thwarted just once and you'll see a different side of them; that's my prediction."

"Well, I don't think that having whatever they desire is the only difference between them and me," I protested. "I'm not a glutton. I wouldn't have eaten so much if I hadn't felt the need to be polite."

"That may be; but we didn't deny ourselves chocolate frosting when we desired it, did we?"

"What about Dido?" I asked, changing the subject. "What kind of love does she feel for me? How can she think she loves me when she pleads for me to remain here, knowing that for me to remain would mean certain death?"

"I can see you know a lot about love! Dido's love is the desire to possess. It's what many people really feel when they think they feel love."

"When did you become an expert in love?" I scoffed.

"Strange as it seems, Pinocchio, I understand the human heart a lot better now that I'm an insect. I came to know good and evil all at once, it seems, when we fell with the cake. And I see that what many people call love is only selfish desire."

Now it was my turn to reply thoughtfully. "If you're right, Gregorio, why do we want to become real boys? We'll live longer, but we won't be any better. No, don't tell me; I can answer my own question. A real boy can find salvation and eternal life. Father, Giuseppe, and so many others in our village know the Lord. I wonder why everyone doesn't turn to Him for salvation. He promises salvation to everyone who comes to Christ in faith, no matter how bad he's been."

"Perhaps they don't believe in God; perhaps they don't believe that God, if He exists, wants to save them. Perhaps they think they're no better than an insect like me. I can't imagine why God would care for a wriggling bug. If I ever become a boy again I hope

I'll have faith to believe that the Lord offers salvation to boys like me, boys who never cared to know or obey him before. But I don't have that faith yet. Where does faith come from, Pinocchio?"

I didn't have an answer to Gregorio's question, and I was too tired to continue the discussion anyway. I put my friend's cage on the table by the window, went to bed, and tried to fall asleep.

Chapter 17

I was still awake at midnight. I had never lain down on a softer bed, but I couldn't sleep. I felt in my wooden bones that something was very wrong in the Avaro villa. When I could watch moonbeams creep across the ceiling no longer, I arose and slipped out of my room. I walked down one dark corridor after another, seeing and hearing nothing. The villa was very large, very quiet, and very dark.

I decided to make another attempt at sleeping and started back towards the bedroom wing. I was near my room, padding soundlessly along the carpeted passage, when I saw a crack of light under a bedroom door. I paused by the door, wondering who else was up at that dead hour. Then I heard voices. I recognized one voice as Dido; the other voice was that of a woman I didn't know. I put my ear to the keyhole.

"Are you sure you can cast a spell on a wooden boy?" I heard Dido ask. "He's not flesh and blood like others you've enchanted."

"Don't you worry about that, Signorina," replied the other voice. "I've cast love spells on more young men than I can remember; I know just what to do. As for his being wooden, remember that I've also cast spells on wells, rocks, houses, and trees. If I can enchant trees I can certainly enchant something made from a tree. Trust me: by this time tomorrow your beloved will be sleeplessly pacing the corridors of this villa thinking of only you. He'll forget his hopeless quest entirely; you alone will fill his thoughts. He'll love you more than life itself."

"You must succeed," Dido said fiercely. "I refuse to be denied anything I desire, and I desire Pinocchio for my husband. I'll make you a rich woman if you get me what I want. I *always* get what I want. How *do* you propose to cast a spell on him?"

"Tomorrow you must see to it that the kitchen maid doesn't report for work. I'll take her place. When the cook isn't looking, I'll cast a love spell on a piece of fruit, a glass of wine, or some other food or drink I find at hand. Pinocchio will fall in love with the first person he looks at after partaking of it. I'll tell you beforehand what the enchanted food or drink is; it will be up to you to make sure that the first person he sees after taking it is you."

Suddenly, the voice of the enchantress spoke from very near the door: "I must go now. I'll return tomorrow morning." I ducked behind a suit of armor standing nearby. The door opened and for a brief moment I could see feet in the lighted doorway; then the door closed and the corridor was black again. I peaked out from behind the armor. The dark outline of a woman in a shawl glided down the corridor and descended the staircase at the end of the wing. I heard the main door close softly. Turning back, I saw the light under Dido's door go out. She had blown out her lamp and gone to bed.

I returned to my room shaken and afraid. Gathering our belongings together, I woke Gregorio.

"Gregorio, we've got to get out of here before morning. Our darling little Dido has called in a witch to cast a spell on me so that I'll fall in love with her." His eyes got as big as a hundred saucers as I told him the witch's plan. When I had finished speaking, Gregorio replied.

"Pinocchio, we can't get out of here before morning. Look out the window."

I looked down at the grounds surrounding the villa. The full moon revealed at least four dark forms prowling the lawns and gardens. Of course! Signor Avaro had let the mastiffs out at night to protect the estate. If I tried to flee they would reduce me to splinters before I got halfway to the gate. A blanket of dread settled down on me, and cold sweat would have stood in beads on my brow if Gepetto had not made me out of dry, well-seasoned wood.

Gregorio saw the fear on my face. "This is a time to use our wits again, Pinocchio, not a time to panic. This time I have the plan; this time I will rescue *you*. Tomorrow morning I'll find a quiet place on the kitchen hearth and wait for the witch to come. I'll see her cast her spell; then I'll tell you so you can refuse the enchanted food or drink. Not a bad plan, eh?"

"Not a bad plan? It's a brilliant plan!" I exclaimed. My sense of doom evaporated like mist in the morning sun. Then the chocolate started to burble softly.

"If we put our heads together," I said, "maybe we can make your plan even better." We spent an hour discussing Gregorio's plan. By the time we had stopped talking I knew what I would do with the enchanted food. I blew out the candle and lay back on the bed. For the first time that night it felt soft and inviting, and I fell asleep immediately. I slept peacefully and awoke refreshed before daybreak. I took Gregorio down to the kitchen; then I returned to my room and slept two hours more.

The custom in great country houses is for guests to rise and breakfast whenever they wish. I rose at eight o'clock and went down to the dining room. Freshly baked rolls, marmalade, and cheese were laid out on the sideboard beside a silver coffee urn. I was wary of eating or drinking anything until I was sure it was safe. Alberto was in the dining room drawing the drapes, so I greeted him and began to make small talk.

"I am glad to see breakfast prepared already," I remarked to the butler. "The cook and the kitchen maid must have gotten up at sunrise to have everything ready at this hour."

"Oh, I lay out breakfast, Signor. The cook prepares breakfast at seven, but Maria does not begin her chores till noon. Signor Avaro sometimes breakfasts at this hour, but Signorina Avaro never rises till after ten." Reassured by Alberto's remarks, especially by the news that Dido had not yet risen, I took breakfast.

I thought then that Gregorio and I might be able to leave before Dido appeared; but when I told Signor Avaro that we really had to continue on our way he wouldn't hear of it.

"But you cannot go until you say goodbye to Dido! She admires you so for your noble soul. Please stay for dinner. We can eat at one o'clock instead of two so you can get an earlier start; and I will have Alberto drive you to Casale after we dine."

Casale was nearly fifteen miles from Vercelli, a good day's walk. If we accepted Signor Avaro's hospitality we would be closer to Genoa by sundown than if I insisted on leaving immediately. Our plan was in place, and I had a few ideas of my own that I had not even told Gregorio. I thought it would be safe to accept Signor Avaro's offer.

"Once more I am indebted to you for your generosity, Signor," I replied in honeyed tones.

"It goes without saying that I won't leave until I say goodbye to your charming daughter. I shall certainly stay for dinner; and I would be most appreciative of a ride to Casale." I felt my nose lengthen as I said those words, but Signor Avaro, who was extremely nearsighted and wore spectacles as thick as melon rind, seemed not to notice.

Chapter 17

I went to walk in the garden before dinner, for I wanted to see the witch when she arrived. I found a bench in an arbor with a clear view of the gate and sat down. I didn't have to wait long before the bell rang. Dido came running up the path to let the caller in. She opened the gate and a woman entered.

The woman had to be the witch, but she wasn't at all what I expected. She was young and beautiful, almost as lovely as Gabriela. A mass of golden curls tumbled out from under her shawl. Her skin was smooth and her complexion was fair, her eyes were green and her full lips were scarlet. But the witch's scarlet mouth was hard; it didn't smile softly like Gabriela's. Her green eyes glared fiercely; they didn't dance like Gabriela's.

Dido and the witch passed the arbor without seeing me and entered the house. Soon I could hear Dido in the garden again, calling my name.

"Pinocchio, where are you? Your Dido is looking for you."

I got up and went towards the voice. I found her in a pretty little sunken rose garden that was in full flower.

"Pinocchio! I've been looking all over for you. I hope you slept well last night."

"Oh, yes," I replied, "I wouldn't have believed a bed could be so soft."

"Dear Pinocchio, you could sleep on a bed like that every night for the rest of your brief life if you would consent to stay here with us. Please reconsider your decision to go to Genoa. No one there can make you a real boy; you'll find only trouble and disappointment. And I can't bear to lose you; I must have you."

I explained again that, as much as I liked and respected her, I had to try to escape the fate awaiting me. I swore again that I would surely return to her when I was flesh and blood. My nose grew again and Dido, who was not nearsighted, noticed. She laughed.

"Pinocchio, your nose just grew a half inch before my eyes!"

"Yes, I felt it," I replied. "It's happened before. I'm powerless to prevent it. I suppose it will be a foot long by the time I'm old enough to marry. No girl who knew about it would want me. I should have told you about it before. No doubt this discovery changes your feelings about me; yes?"

"You don't know much about girls, do you, Pinocchio; certainly not much about a girl like me. When I want something, the desire takes on a life of its own. When I was a very little girl, I wanted my friend's puppy. I whined and cried and threw a tantrum until my father offered her father a lot of money. The man was poor, so he sold his daughter's pet. My friend cried for days, she loved that puppy so.

"Well, the puppy grew up into the ugliest dog in Vercelli. I no longer wanted to play with it or even look at it, but I wouldn't give it back to my friend, who truly loved it. She never spoke to me after that, but I didn't care. I got what I wanted and wouldn't give it up even when I didn't want it anymore."

Dido stopped talking, sensing that she had said more than she wanted. At that moment Alberto called us to dinner. Dido excused herself to dress for dinner. I knew she would go first to the kitchen to talk with the witch. I hurried back to the house to find out what Gregorio had discovered. When I reached my room I was relieved to see Gregorio squatting on the floor by the door. I picked him up and went into the room. After I carefully closed the door, I asked him what he learned in the kitchen.

"What an enchanting woman is that witch, Pinocchio! What a beauty! If I had not been told she was a witch I would never have suspected it. How true is the saying: Beauty is only skin deep. People aren't always what they seem, are they? Or animals either, for that matter."

"The spell, Gregorio! This is no time to talk philosophy! On what did she cast the spell?"

"I'm coming to that. That beautiful, evil woman put a pinch of white powder in one of the wine glasses. The powder will dissolve in the wine. As soon as you drink the wine you'll fall in love with the first person you see. I'm sure that at this very minute she's telling Dido to be sure you're looking at her when you take your first sip of wine."

"How can I identify the glass? They all looked the same last night."

"They all look the same today too. Perhaps it has a chip or some other marking I couldn't see. But you can be sure it will be that glass and no other that will be given to you."

"Good work, friend; I'll be on my guard. By the way, I'm taking you to dinner with me. You'll amuse and distract the little signorina and her father. That will help me with my plan."

"What do you mean, your plan?" asked Gregorio, alarmed. "Your aim tonight is to avoid the witch's spell; that's all. Don't complicate things. Haven't we learned by now that we aren't nearly as clever as we thought when we first set out on our quest?"

"Haven't we learned by now that we can escape the most dangerous pickle by using our wits?" I retorted. "Don't worry; I'm not going to do anything stupid."

With that I wiped my wooden face and hands with a washrag, tucked in my shirt tail, fastened Gregorio's cage to my belt, and went down to dinner.

Alberto seated me next to Dido, as before; Signor Avaro sat at the head of the table. When Alberto began to serve the food the witch appeared in a maid's uniform with the wine.

"Where is Maria, Alberto?" asked Signor Avaro.

"She is ill, Signor," Alberto answered. "This is her cousin, Fata, who happens to be visiting. Signorina Dido asked her to take Maria's place until she is well again."

Fata smiled and curtseyed. She set glasses before us and filled them with wine from a carafe; then she retired to the kitchen.

It was time to act. I put Gregorio on the table.

"I haven't had the opportunity to show you how talented my cricket is," I said. "You've seen only a few of his tricks. Since I'll be leaving after dinner I brought him to the table to perform for you now. Gregorio, hop to the foot of the table and sing for us." Gregorio looked at me with a hundred wary eyes and didn't move. "Go on," I said in a firm voice, "Show these people of quality what you can do."

Gregorio obediently leaped over all the dishes and candles in a single bound and landed at the far end of the table. As the eyes of Dido and Signor Avaro followed Gregorio in flight I exchanged wineglasses with Dido. Her eyes were fixed on Gregorio and my slight-of-hand went undetected.

Gregorio began to sing a Neapolitan ballad. "Bravo! Bravo!" cried Signor Avaro. Dido laughed and glanced at me. I was clapping vigorously—she could see that I wouldn't be drinking for the moment. She picked up her glass and turned her eyes back to the singing cricket. As I continued clapping, Dido raised the glass to her lips and drained it in a single gulp, still watching Gregorio. I stopped clapping and began to sip my wine quietly. It mingled delightfully with the chocolate swirling inside.

Gregorio obediently leaped over all the dishes and candles in a single bound and landed at the far end of the table. As the eyes of Dido and Signor Avaro followed Gregorio, I exchanged wineglasses with Dido.

Chapter 17

The look on Dido's face changed from merriment to rapture all in a moment.

"Father, what a handsome cricket!" she exclaimed. "Look how his metallic black body shines in the candlelight! What noble antennae crown his head! And his eyes, Father! Every one of them reflects the many colors of the rainbow—no, they glow from within, showing the radiance of his soul! Father, for the first time in my life I am truly in love. I love this cricket passionately, with all my heart."

Signor Avaro was too shocked to reply. His jaw dropped and his mouth gaped, revealing a jumbled mix of gold and rotten teeth. A thin trickle of saliva started down from the corner of his mouth. Alberto tried to look expressionless, as a good butler should, but the blood drained from his face and his hands began to tremble.

Dido turned to me and smiled softly, pity in her eyes.

"Pinocchio, I realize now that what I felt for you was only childish infatuation. Please forgive me for hurting you like this, but my heart belongs to your cricket. I can never be happy until he is mine. You wouldn't stand in the way of my happiness, would you? Sell him to me. Father will pay whatever you ask, won't you, Father dear?"

I quickly spoke up. "Signor Avaro, I think we should have a private word in the hall right away."

"Yes, yes; right away," muttered Dido's father. "Alberto, the signorina isn't well. Stay with her and see to it that she doesn't do something that would, uh, endanger her health further." He rose and went quickly into the hall.

"What do you mean, endanger my health further?" cried Dido. "You all think I'm crazy, don't you? There's nothing wrong with me except that I'm sick with love. That's normal for a young girl, isn't it? Yes, I'm sick with love for this most talented, most noble, most handsome insect. Your little minds cannot conceive of such a love, but my love for this cricket is deeper and purer than any love you'll ever know. I must make this darling insect mine!" With those words Dido stood up and lunged with outstretched arms towards Gregorio.

"Gregorio!" I cried, and held out my hand. My friend jumped over Dido and landed on my palm. I ran to join Signor Avaro in the hall while Alberto held Dido down in her chair. I could hear her shrieking as I closed the dining room door.

"Signor," I said, as soon as I had joined Dido's father in the hall, "I have no idea what has come over your poor daughter. Perhaps she sat in the sun with me too long this morning." Of course, my nose grew as I told this lie, but Signor Avaro was in no condition to notice.

"I must take my cricket and leave here right now," I continued. "I am sure dear Dido will be better in the morning, but for me to remain here with Gregorio even another quarter-hour would upset her dangerously. There's no telling what she might do while she's unbalanced. It would help Dido greatly if Alberto drove us to Casale as you offered—the more distance between her and my pet, the better. We must get so far away so fast that even in her deranged state she realizes that it would be hopeless to try to find us. You could get one of the other servants to guard her while Alberto gets the horse and cart ready."

"You are as wise as you are noble, Pinocchio," said my host. "I will give the necessary orders at once. All will be ready for your departure in ten minutes." Signor Avaro turned and walked rapidly (for a man of his bulk) towards the servants' quarters.

I expected Gregorio to rebuke me severely for the trick I had played on Dido but he only said, "We'll have to talk about this when we're safely away, Pinocchio."

Signor Avaro was as good as his word. In exactly ten minutes Alberto knocked on my door just as I was tying the last knot in my blanket roll. He carried a basket, which he handed to me.

"The master ordered me to pack something for you to eat on the way to Casale."

"Did you pack this lunch with your own hands or did that woman Fata prepare it?" I asked.

"I prepared the basket, sir. Signor Avaro told Fata to take care of Signorina Dido."

"Then let's not waste a minute, Alberto," I replied. "To be perfectly frank, I don't think Fata will be any help to the poor signorina. I wouldn't be at all surprised if that woman actually encourages the little signorina to pursue us."

Alberto looked at me with questioning eyes but said nothing. We climbed into the coach and were quickly off. Alberto laid the whip on the horses' backs with a will and we reached Casale in an hour. I barely had time to finish the delicious lunch he had prepared before we came in sight of the city.

Chapter 18

The road from Vercelli ran due south to a ferry on the north bank of the Po. I could see the roofs and towers of Casale directly across the river, climbing the opposite bank like some scaly creature emerging from the water.

"This is as far as I take you, Signor," said Alberto, reining in the horses at the ferry landing. "I must return to Signorina Dido immediately. I don't trust that woman Fata any more than you do. God bless you on your journey, Signor."

Alberto helped me down from the coach, bowing to me as though I were a real gentleman. Climbing back on the bench, he snapped the reins and wheeled the coach about. The horses bolted forward, the coach vanished in the dust and heat of the road, and I was alone with Gregorio.

"Well, Gregorio, we've reached the Po safe and well."

"Yes, Pinocchio. We must give thanks to God for delivering us from that selfish little girl and that beautiful, dangerous enchantress. Did you know she was the famous witch, Fata Morgana?"

Young as I was, I had heard of Fata Morgana. From the Alps to Sicily, the name of Fata Morgana struck fear into the hearts of young and old alike.

"Fata Morgana!" I exclaimed. "And to think I was so proud of my scheme! I've been thinking myself more clever than ever, but now I see that my wits would have profited nothing if God hadn't granted us success. We must indeed thank him for delivering us from the clutches of that fiend."

We bowed our heads right there and thanked God for rescuing us from Dido and Fata. People walking on the road looked at us sideways as they passed but I didn't care. For a brief moment the chocolate inside was quiet, and I could see clearly that God had managed our escape.

We walked down the grassy bank to the water's edge. The ferry wasn't there. A boy about my age—that is, the age I appeared to be—was fishing from the end of the dock. I walked out to the boy and asked him when the ferry would be back. He said it would return about three o'clock if the water was not too rough.

The water looked rough to me. Gusty winds were kicking up whitecaps on the wide river, eddies curled and uncurled on the water's surface, and long swells rolled in to shore. The sky was growing darker minute by minute; tall thunderheads rose and flattened out into anvils as I stood on the landing looking up at the angry heavens.

With the first crack of thunder, I ran back to land looking for shelter from the downpour that would begin any minute. A decrepit skiff lay keel up on the bank and I scrambled underneath just in time. In a minute, rain was streaming off the sides of the skiff and running in rivulets down the bank to the river. Plenty of water found its way into my sanctuary through cracks in the rotten hull.

I draped my blanket over my head and huddled under it to wait out the cloudburst. At least the ferry wouldn't come and go without us; it would wait on the opposite bank until the storm was over. As the rain drummed on the bottom of my shelter I began to talk to Gregorio. "Very well, conscience of mine; go ahead and tell me I shouldn't have tricked Dido like that."

"You were playing with fire, Pinocchio, when you exchanged glasses with Dido, and we may still rue the day. When you outwitted Dido you also foiled Fata Morgana. That witch won't rest till she finds you and visits some horrible punishment on you.

"And what about me?" he continued. "Now little Dido is infatuated with me and wants me for her own. She'll search for me night and day. They know you were making for Casale. You can be sure that Dido and Fata Morgana have already left the villa and are on their way here. I tell you, they'll pursue us to the ends of the earth.

"But that's not the worst of it," my friend went on. "What would your father say? What would Barbe Filippo say? They would tell you not to return evil for evil. And that's not their own idea of what's right: the Lord taught that very thing, didn't he? You told me so yourself the time I got back at Paolo Busseto for getting me in trouble with Don Camillo, the priest.

"You really made a mess of things, you woodenhead. You entered Vercelli determined to please the Lord and do good; that was why you helped the beggar. You left Vercelli having brought a life-long curse on Signorina Avaro. Bad as she is, she didn't deserve that; and even if she did, we should leave such things up to God.

"There, I've had my say. Think about it, please, and in the future resist the temptation to give back more evil than you got. Returning evil for evil is still doing evil."

"Everything you say is true, Gregorio," I confessed. "But the chocolate inside me churned and welled up so, I couldn't help myself—I didn't even want to help myself. I have to admit that, as much as I know it's wrong, the thought of Dido hopelessly in love with an insect gives me pleasure.

"Do you think if we ever become real boys we'll love the good and the noble and hate the bad and the despicable?"

"Not at all," Gregorio replied. "Think about all the boys in our little village. They're no better than a wooden boy or an insect as far as loving the good and hating the bad is concerned. I tell you, Pinocchio, we need to be born again, as Barbe Filippo preaches.

"But why go on talking like this? We need to become real boys first, and I'm losing hope that we'll ever reach our goal."

"God must care for us, Gregorio, in spite of our deviltry: if He didn't care He would have left us at the mercy of that terrible witch. He has brought us through so many dangers already; I have to believe he intends to give us success."

"Well, well; for once you aren't crowing about how your wits got you out of a jam. That's an improvement."

We would have gone on talking about the Lord and human nature and fate and other deep things for a long time, but by then the rain had stopped. I crawled out from under the boat and blinked in the fresh sunshine. Looking across the river, I saw the ferry begin its trip back to our side. It would be here soon. I wrung out my blanket, which was quite wet, and rolled it around my belongings again.

The ferry arrived from the city and a dozen people got off: three country women who had sold eggs, eggplant, or who knows what in the market and were returning home with a few coins; two nuns dressed in thick, black habits who nevertheless looked quite cool; four soldiers on leave, going home to the farm for mother's cooking; and three solitary travelers who looked like they had many miles yet to go.

The ferryman collected five lire from me and told me I would have to wait for a half-hour or until he had a dozen passengers. I sat down in the bow and waited. Presently a large, shapeless woman in a polka dot dress dragged two squirming children into the boat and sat down behind me. By the time a half-hour passed we had been joined by a pair of priests, a farmer with a chicken in a cage, and two well-fed soldiers making their way back to barracks.

The ferryman was about to cast off and begin the trip over to the city when we heard voices shouting at him to wait. Looking over my shoulder, I saw Dido and Fata Morgana running down the landing! I turned my head quickly and slumped down behind the bulky form of the woman in the polka dot dress. I didn't think they had seen me.

Fully loaded, the boat moved slowly away from the dock as the ferryman energetically worked his oar back and forth. We were exactly in the middle of the river when a flash of lightning split the sky right over the city. Another storm was coming our way. I watched the dark clouds move steadily towards us, dropping their curtain of rain as they advanced. When the wall of wind and rain hit us the river came alive. It seethed and boiled and heaved. Water began to spray into the boat.

My thoughts were on the storm when an icy hand gripped my shoulder and spun me around. I found myself face to face with Dido and the witch. Fata Morgana had the ferryman's iron gaff in her hand. Lightning flashed off its three sharp points as she shook it over my head.

I found myself face to face with Dido and the witch. Fata Morgana had the ferryman's iron gaff in her hand.

Chapter 19

I blurted out the first thing that came to mind: "Put that hook down or I'll jump in the river. I'm made of wood, remember? I can't sink. If you were so foolish as to follow me the churning waters would swallow you up before you could blink an eye."

The witch stopped the gaff in mid-swing and stood frozen like a statue, eyes burning with silent hate. Dido pushed her aside and we stood face to face. She clutched a fat purse in her chubby hand.

"We don't want to hurt you, Pinocchio," she screamed above the howling wind. "We've come to fetch your divine cricket back to Vercelli. I must have him; I don't care about you. Turn my beloved over to me and all will be well. This purse is stuffed with a thousand gold ducats. They're yours if you sell me your darling pet."

"Gregorio is my friend, not my pet! I would never sell my friend! But he did confess to me that he grew very fond of you during our stay. Maybe he's in love with you, too, and would return to Vercelli of his own free will. Let me discuss the matter with him privately, puppet to cricket."

Dido and the witch withdrew to the middle of the ferry; I turned away and crouched down again in the bow. The crashing waves chilled my wooden body to its very core of Milano steel. I gritted my teeth to stop their chattering and drew the little wicker cage out from under my blanket, which I had wrapped around my body in a vain effort to keep out the drenching rain and waves.

"Quick, out of the cage and into my hat. We're going to play one last trick on this wicked pair." Gregorio crawled into my hat without a word of protest. He really had no choice but to go along with whatever I had in mind, for even if he had objected he could never have made himself heard over the roar of the storm.

I turned and motioned for Dido and Fata Morgana to come forward. "Gregorio agrees to go back with you if you give me the money," I lied. Rain was streaming off my nose and they didn't seem to notice that it grew another quarter-inch on the spot.
I passed the cage to Dido and snatched the purse in one quick motion. I leapt up on the gunwale, preparing to jump overboard, just as the witch swung the gaff at my head. I caught the shaft with

my free hand but the blow knocked me off balance. I tumbled into the surging river, pulling the witch with me.

We rose to the surface together. Somehow the witch had managed to get a grip on the purse. The astonished passengers gaped dumbly as we struggled to keep afloat, each of us gripping the gaff with one hand and the purse with the other, spluttering, gasping, and kicking furiously to keep our heads above the choppy waves. Fata Morgana was stronger than any man I'd ever met; I couldn't wrench the money or the hook away from her. I didn't dare let go of the gaff and I wouldn't give up the money, but all that iron and gold was pulling me under.

"Let the purse go, Pinocchio," squeaked Gregorio in panic. "You can't make it to shore with all that gold weighing you down; it will drag us under in the end." I knew my friend was right but I couldn't give up all that gold—greed held me in a grip far, far stronger than my grip on the purse. I kept kicking and flailing my elbows in a losing struggle with the river. I was going down.

But before I slipped completely below the waves a fiery blow struck the knuckles of my left hand, the one clutching the purse. Numbed with pain, my fingers relaxed their grip for an instant. Fata Morgana jerked the gold and the gaff away from me and smiled in triumph; then her smile twisted into an expression of horror as the heavy purse dragged her beneath the waves. I never saw her again.

I looked to the boat: what had struck the blow that saved my life? I tell you, nothing could have surprised me more than what I saw at that moment: Gabriela stood in the boat, a shepherd's staff in her hand! Before I had the wit to speak a large wave picked me up and swept me away. The vision of my beloved dissolved in spray and driving rain.

I was at the mercy of the wild river, but freed from the purse, I couldn't sink. I floated with wind and current until the storm passed over city and river, roaring north towards Vercelli and the Alps. The wind gentled, the waves flattened, and I was able to swim to the southern bank.

I dragged myself to my feet and looked around. I was only a mile downstream from Casale. I stumped up the sloping dike as quickly as I could, water dripping from my clothing and squishing in my shoes. A road ran along the top of the dike, and I made for the city as fast as my swollen joints would let me.

Fata Morgana jerked the gold and the gaff away from me and smiled in triumph; then her smile twisted into an expression of horror as the heavy purse dragged her beneath the waves. I never saw her again.

"Aren't you even going to look to see if I survived this ordeal, Pinocchio?" asked an impatient voice.

"I'm sorry, Gregorio," I said, and kept walking briskly towards town. "Honestly, I forgot you were with me. Gabriela was on that ferry! I didn't see her get on, did you? She had a shepherd's staff, of all things, which she used to knock that purse right out of my hand. We've got to get to the ferry landing and find her."

"You won't find her, Pinocchio. You didn't see Gabriela, you saw an angel sent by the Lord God to save you from your own sin and foolishness. Left to your greed you would be dead and waterlogged at the bottom of the river, still clutching that purse. The first idea you had when you saw Dido and Fata was the best one. All you had to do was jump in the water; but no, you had to be clever and try to get the money, too. Dido's gold would have pulled us to destruction if the Lord had not sent the angel Gabriele to save us. Your love didn't get on the ferry with the other passengers and she won't be on it when the boat docks. Take my word for it, you saw a real angel."

"Gregorio, I saw a real girl. I've called Gabriela an angel many times, but that's only a figure of speech."

"We'll have to talk about it some other time," said my friend, who had moved to the peak of my cap to get a better view of things. "Right now you'd better find a place to hide. I hear the voice of that bewitched little rich girl up ahead."

I stopped and strained my ears. Our dousing hadn't dulled Gregorio's antennae. No one could mistake that high piping voice for another's: none other than Dido was coming our way.

"Gregorio, my love! Pinocchio! Where are you? Have you reached shore safely? My darling cricket, tell me you're all right!"

I flattened my body against the nearest tree—fortunately, it was a large one—and peeked out from behind the trunk. Dido came into view walking slowly along the river's edge, scanning the shore and shallows and calling our names every minute. She must have expected to find us lying battered and senseless in some eddy; not once did she glance up at the top of the dike.

As soon as Dido passed out of sight I sprang from my hiding place and ran all the way to the ferry landing. Our fellow passengers had already scattered. The ferry was ready to return to the northern shore and the boatman was in the very act of casting off the mooring line. I sprinted down the bank, yelling at him to wait. The man was dumbfounded to see me again but recovered himself and congratulated me on the happy occasion of managing to survive my ordeal.

"Where is the angel with the shepherd's staff, the one who struck my hand and saved my life?" I asked, ignoring his well-intended words.

"Why, Signor, that was the first marvelous thing that happened on your passage across the river," he replied, "the second being your entirely unexpected but happy appearance after I had given you up for dead. As for your question, I have no idea where the beautiful signorina came from or where she went. I know I didn't take her fare or help her into the boat; but in the middle of the river I blinked, and there she was, sitting beside me in the stern! Before I could ask her how she came to be there, you fell into the water and I forgot all about her while we watched you struggle with that other woman. I saw the young lady touch your hand with her staff—she didn't strike it. Then you were swept away. I was sure you had drowned. I turned to the beautiful signorina, but she had disappeared—simply vanished! Nothing like this has ever happened to me in my dull life. It's all very wonderful and mysterious."

I collected my soggy belongings and Gregorio's cage from the bow and trudged thoughtfully up the bank towards the city. Neither of us spoke until we had passed through the city gate; then Gregorio, who must have been reading my thoughts, broke the silence.

"Don't forget the quest, Pinocchio. You have less than six months to live. We've got to press on to Genoa right away. Why, we're almost halfway there. You left Gabriela to go on this quest for life; don't spend precious time looking for her now. If it was really she who saved us, she'll find us when we need her."

The great clock in the city hall struck five as Gregorio was speaking. We would have to stay the night in Casale. I didn't feel completely at ease there, for Dido was sure to spend the night in the city, too. Fortunately, Casale had more than a dozen inns. I chose a run-down establishment in a humble part of town where Dido would never stoop to go.

My choice was a happy one. We dined in the commons that evening and enjoyed a restful night behind locked doors. The next morning we rose, ate breakfast, paid our bill, and left town before eight o'clock. We saw nothing of Dido.

Chapter 20

The air was cool and fresh when we left Casale. Our destination was Alessandria, twenty miles south. If it stayed cool we would reach Alessandria by nightfall, but if the weather turned muggy again I would be exhausted by early afternoon and we would be forced to stop short of our goal. I prayed for cool weather. I had to reach Genoa and find Doctor Moro before I ran down, and every day was precious to me.

We were both in a mood to talk after the excitement of the previous day. Gregorio began our conversation.

"There are many lessons to be learned from all we went through yesterday, Pinocchio."

"Yes," I replied. "The first is that God uses the very forces of nature to punish evil. Fata Morgana was far quicker than I, but all her cunning could not outwit wind, water, and gravity. She sank like a stone."

"I disagree, Pinocchio. The first lesson is that we don't learn our lessons the first time. Not thirty minutes after agreeing that you wouldn't return evil for evil, you tried to cheat Dido out of that purse of gold."

"She offered to buy you for money, Gregorio, like a common barnyard animal! She deserved to lose that money. God gave me an opportunity to teach that spoiled little girl a lesson. I was clever enough to see a way to teach her that lesson and to profit from it as well. It was a brilliant plan even if I did almost drown."

"Your words prove my point about the first lesson, Pinocchio, but to drive it home let's talk about another lesson you didn't learn the first time. You aren't nearly as clever as you think. You may have fooled Dido when you gave her my empty cage and took her purse but Fata Morgana wasn't fooled. She nearly brained you with the gaff."

"I won't argue with you there; but my baptism in the Po taught me something about myself that will keep me out of trouble in the future. I was carried away by greed. When the chocolate inside me boils, vapors of greed, pride, and anger rise up and cloud my brain. I knew I couldn't outwit Fata Morgana, but when I saw that purse heavy with gold, I forgot everything I knew and behaved like a fool. It was as if I knew the danger but just didn't care.

"Even Fata Morgana, quick as she was, was blinded by her sin. She could have let the money and that murderous hook go, but she would not, and they pulled her down. As the Sicilians say, now she sleeps with the fishes. I've learned from all this, Gregorio; I've learned to beware of the sin within me."

"Pinocchio, how can this knowledge keep you out of trouble? When the chocolate begins to boil you won't care that it's sin rising within you. You'll stifle those warnings just as you did when you matched wits with the witch."

"Perhaps you're right; maybe I'm not strong enough to resist temptation. Very well then, I know what I must do. I'll be very, very good when the chocolate isn't boiling up. If I'm good enough then, God will overlook my failings later. I believe that if my good deeds outweigh my bad ones God will look with favor on me and make me a real boy."

"It seems to me that God saved your neck out of the goodness of His heart," Gregorio shot back. "If that beautiful angel hadn't smashed your knuckles you would have held on to that gold though it meant your life. God sent an angel to save you, but you're no angel."

"Gregorio, when God helps us without our deserving it at all, just out of the goodness of His heart, that's what Barbe Filippo calls grace. But grace is for those who need it. It wasn't out of grace that the Lord rescued me. I admit that God sent Gabriela to save my life, but I deserved to be rescued. I am a good puppet, a gentle and kind-hearted puppet, every bit as good as many real boys you and I know. In fact, I'm better than most of them. I haven't done very much that's bad, and most of that was in getting even with wicked people who mistreated me first. That can't be wrong: God helps those who help themselves, even when they're getting even."

"Well, I can see there's no arguing with you now," said my friend. "But grace is what I need even if you can do without it. I don't believe Doctor Moro or any other man has the power to turn a bug into a boy. God could do it if he felt gracious towards me, but I don't have any reason to expect that. I don't claim to be so good that God must save me, like some blockheads I know. I need grace, but I don't have much faith that the Lord has grace for me."

Chapter 20

It was time to change the subject. We just didn't see eye to eye. Besides, I didn't want Gregorio to fall into the deep melancholy that seemed to seize him now and again. But just then we rounded a bend in the road and came upon a scene so extraordinary that we entirely forgot what we were talking about.

A richly dressed traveler was standing in the middle of the road. He wore a crimson silk scarf knotted at the neck. A heavy belt was wrapped tightly around his slender waist. Well-tailored trousers cut from soft gray wool and sturdy black riding boots completed the traveler's outfit.

It wasn't the man's attire that stopped us in our tracks; we had met with wealthier travelers since leaving home. What captured our attention was the fine shotgun he held in his hands. The stock was exquisitely carved red oak, wrought with such skill that only a craftsman equal to Giuseppe or Gepetto could have fashioned it. The breech and barrel were made of fine steel intricately engraved with curlicues, fruits, and leaves; the engraving was inlaid with gold. The most striking feature of this scene was that the man was pointing the shotgun straight at my chest and shouting angrily, "Prepare to die!"

"Don't shoot, Signor!" I cried. "We're not robbers, but travelers like yourself. Have mercy!"

The man lowered his gun and smiled broadly. "Excuse me for frightening you, young man. I wasn't pointing this shotgun at you; I was about to shoot that miserable nag behind you."

I turned around. A bay mare stood motionless behind me in the grassy strip between the road and the neighboring field. I had walked right by the beast without noticing her, so still did she stand and so absorbed had I been in our conversation. The horse didn't look old; her back was straight and she was long in tooth. But she stood with bowed neck, trembling and soaked with sweat, her spirit broken as if she had been an old dobbin whipped for years by some brutish peasant.

A second look told me that her spirit was not completely broken. The mare's eyes smoldered with defiance as well as defeat. She knew her master had doomed her to die, and to death she would submit, but she would not submit to him.

Those eyes kindled curiosity and pity in my mechanical soul. "If I may ask, Signor, why are you preparing to kill this beast? She doesn't look sick or injured."

"She refuses to go a step further. I don't understand it. I bought the animal six months ago and she carried me willingly until today. But not an hour ago, while I was grazing my beasts right here, one of my pack animals slipped her tether and ran away. I was forced to load my goods on my saddle horse—this wicked creature! Now she refuses to move. She has seen me whip my pack animals into line often enough; you would think she would fear to disobey—yet she won't budge! I'm going to shoot her as an example to my other horses. When they see how I deal with open rebellion they'll obey without question, you can bet! Now if you'll stand out of the way, please, I'll dispatch this piece of ungrateful carrion."

"Wait, Signor!" I said quickly, smiling sweetly. "I have a proposition for you. Let me buy this cantankerous beast. I'm an animal trainer; with time I can subdue her will. Look, I have a trained cricket here. If I can train a cricket I can train anything, even a worthless nag like your horse."

I had Gregorio do some somersaults on the palm of my hand to demonstrate the remarkable ability with animals I had claimed. Gregorio caught on to my plan right away and performed on command. I didn't have him do anything that might excite the greed of the merchant; we had had enough trouble with people who wanted Gregorio for their own!

The horse's master was agreeable. "Well, young man, I'm willing to sell this stubborn hack to you if you really think you can do something with her, but I warn you that even the threat of death itself isn't enough to make her obey."

"Shall we say five ducats?" I asked, beginning the bargaining.

It wasn't long before the merchant was on his way down the road with six ducats, and Gregorio and I had a horse on our hands.

"Shall we say five ducats?" I asked, beginning the bargaining. It wasn't long before the merchant was on his way down the road with six ducats, and Gregorio and I had a horse on our hands.

Chapter 21

If you think I saved the horse's life because I felt sorry for the beast, you're right; but that wasn't the only reason. We were making slow progress towards Genoa, and the Appenine Mountains lay between us and our goal. We would reach Genoa much sooner if we could ride the rest of the way. I explained my motives to Gregorio, who seemed puzzled by my deed of charity.

"That's all well and good," he replied when I had finished, "but this horse refuses to go anymore. What makes you think you can get her to carry you?"

"Why, it's your job to persuade her," I informed my six-legged friend. Now, I should have told you earlier that when Gregorio was transformed into a cricket he found he could understand the speech of animals. He informs me that all beasts and birds—insects, too—speak a common tongue among themselves, though each kind sounds different to humans and wooden boys. Gregorio could understand the barking of dogs, the mewing of cats, the cooing of pigeons, and the snorting and neighing of horses; and all of them could understand his squeaking and chirping. Do you remember how Gregorio drove Farmer Lavoratore's donkey into a frenzy? He did that with a string of taunts we Flatlanders used to fling at the Mountaineers. We viewed the Mountaineers as donkeys anyway, and Gregorio thought the insults that enraged them would have the same effect on a real donkey. As you know, he succeeded in driving the beast mad.

"Tell the horse that if she carries us to Genoa we will turn her out into the richest pasture in Liguria," I instructed my friend.

"I have to proceed in my own way," Gregorio replied. With that he vaulted to the horse's back, hopped up her neck, and squatted down in front of the beast's left ear, where he began to crick and creak and chirp and squeak. The horse replied with whinnies and snorts and neighs. Back and forth they conversed while I waited impatiently. Finally Gregorio made a flying leap from the horse's head to my shoulder and related the gist of their conversation.

"I had to win her trust first, Pinocchio. I explained that we bought her from her master to set her free."

"You what?" I cried. "Why did you promise that? Now I will have to walk away from this bend in the road on my own two legs, the same way I walked up to it, and we're out six ducats in the bargain."

"Don't sell my wit short. I warned her that if she's found wandering about with no master she'll wind up behind some peasant's plow, if not skinned and drying on his barn door. I explained our quest and invited her to join our party. She has accepted my invitation in the hope that Doctor Moro will turn her into a human being, too. In exchange for a bag of oats every evening and morning she'll let us ride. By the way, our horse calls herself Clover."

I had to admire Gregorio's skill in winning over the stubborn beast. Now we had a horse; Genoa lay ahead. The hot June sun had already dried Clover's coat. I mounted her and shook the reins. Clover wheeled around and began first to walk unsteadily, then to trot with increased confidence down the road.

As we headed south into the mid-morning sun I asked Gregorio what else he had learned from Clover. Why had she refused to carry her master's saddlebags? They were much lighter than the merchant himself.

"Clover is proud, as proud as any queen. To be a rich man's mount was honorable; she lorded it over the other horses. Then her master decided to make her a beast of burden like the rest, and the shame was too much. She resolved to die rather than submit to the humiliation."

"I've heard of men too proud to accept their humble state, but I've never heard of a proud animal."

"You don't know animals very well, Pinocchio. Peacocks are vain, horses and lions are proud, and cats are positively haughty."

"Are you sure, Gregorio? No one could be more servile than Gatto, and he's a cat."

"Yes, but he went to Doctor Moro to be changed into a man. The truly humble accept their condition; the proud want always to go higher. Gatto isn't like us; with him it wasn't a matter of change or die, but pure and simple pride."

"Perhaps you're right, but I hope we never have occasion to find out the true condition of Gatto's heart—may we never see those two rogues again!

As we headed south into the mid-morning sun I asked Gregorio what else he had learned from Clover.

Chapter 21

I bounced up and down on Clover's spine as she jogged steadily south. We reached the Tanaro River in three hours and paused to gaze at the tile roofs of Alessandria on the other bank. A triple arch of yellow brick spanned the river—no need to ferry across here. Clover arched her neck arrogantly and pranced across the bridge as though bearing a victorious general up to the gates of the vanquished.

We did not plan to linger in Alessandria, but to press on towards the south. But it was time for the afternoon *siesta*, so we turned aside to rest in the shade of the city wall. All three of us napped well, waking around four o'clock. We refreshed ourselves with food and drink, then took to the road again. Midsummer's Eve was very near and we had almost five hours of daylight remaining when we left the city. The late afternoon sun was mild, the road was smooth, and the ride was peaceful. For the first time in days nothing happened to us; we simply rode on in silence, enjoying the sights and smells and sounds of the fruitful country around us.

We reached the outskirts of Novi a good hour before the round red sun sank into the western plain. A large guest house just outside the wall had already lit its lanterns to welcome travelers like us, and we decided to stay there for the night. Before seeing to my own accomodations, I led Clover around to the stables to fulfill Gregorio's promise. I soon had her settled in a warm stall, leisurely munching oats out of a full nosebag. Clover told Gregorio how content she was with our agreement. I had him assure her that she would be even more satisfied in a day or two after Doctor Moro had made her a queen.

Gregorio hopped on my hat and squatted down behind the feather; I went into the commons to make arrangements for supper and a room. I made sure the room had thick iron bars over the window. God restored Gregorio to me after Ladrone had kidnapped him, but I didn't want to put the Lord to the test a second time.

After supper I went up to our room. I locked the door and then went to the window to watch the dying of the day. Gregorio jumped down to my shoulder and regarded the scene with me.

The full moon was rising, its soft silver beams replacing the dusky rays of the departing sun.

"This is our last night on the plain, Gregorio. Look off to the south there: Can you see those gray mountains against the dark sky?

They are the Appenines. Tomorrow we'll follow the great southern road as it zig-zags up to the crest of the ridge. By noon we'll be looking down on Genoa and the sea from the top of the pass; tomorrow night we'll sleep in the great city where Columbus was born. Then it's just a matter of finding Doctor Moro. Let's go to bed. I know it's early, but I'm anxious to leave at first light."

I had no idea when I blew out the candle and wrapped my blanket around me that we would rise while the moon was still high in the sky, that our moonlit road would not lead to Genoa, and that I would watch the moon wane and wax again through another window, one guarded by thick iron bars.

Chapter 22

Rough hands dragged me from my warm bed; harsh voices shouted at me. I turned my head away from a lantern that had been shoved under my nose; more rough hands twisted my face back to the painful light. My mind struggled to clear away the cobwebs of sleep. With a shake of my head and a grunt the swirling forms and noise around me fell into order. Squinting into the light, I saw four very unfriendly faces scowling at me. Two men were pressing me against the wall while one of the others held the flaring lantern up to my face.

"Don't worry about due process, lad," a stout, unshaved man laughed. "Your guilt is as plain as the nose on your face—and that's quite a nose—but we'll let the magistrate pass sentence all official-like before we hang you. Novi is a law-abiding town."

"God saw to it that your crime would come to light," said a pale man with pimples. "Of all the towns you could have lodged in, you picked the hometown of Signor Godoti himself. Everyone here knows Clover."

"There's no thief more despicable than a horse thief," spat a black-bearded man. "If I had my way, we wouldn't trouble the magistrate or waste the city's money feeding you, but my friends insist on a trial for you."

"The carabinieri are crawling all over the country, Guido," said an older man who carried himself like the leader of this posse. "Even though they're busy looking for Pietraviva and his cutthroats, we'd be in hot water if we executed this wretch without going through the proper forms. Besides, maybe he's one of Pietraviva's men. We ought to question him. He won't eat that much in jail; Cornelio will see to that. Take him away."

My mind was all too clear now. The merchant who sold us Clover lived in Novi. His townsmen thought I had stolen his horse.

"Just a minute!" I cried. "You've jumped to the wrong conclusion. I met a merchant on the road north of Alessandria—I guess he must have been your friend, Signor Godoti. I bought his horse; I didn't steal her." I told the five men how their friend had been ready

My mind struggled to clear away the cobwebs of sleep. With a shake of my head and a grunt the swirling forms and noise around me fell into order. Squinting into the light, I saw four very unfriendly faces scowling at me.

to shoot Clover and how I bought her for six ducats. "You see," I concluded, "I came by my horse honestly."

The pimply man remained unconvinced. "Godoti would never have sold Clover for six ducats; he's so cheap he'd rather shoot his horse than sell her for such a paltry sum."

"Well, I'm not sure of that," replied the black-bearded man, "but I can't believe that Clover would rather die than carry saddlebags. It looks like we'll have to wait for Godoti to return from his journey; then we can ask him himself."

"But what if this young thief has done him in?" asked the stout man. "I'll bet Godoti is lying dead in some roadside ditch at this very minute."

"Godoti should be back in two weeks," said the leader of the posse. "We'll wait for Godoti. If he doesn't return in a month we'll know he met with foul play at the hands of our suspect here; then we'll bring him before the magistrate. A quick trial and conviction will follow, then a slow hanging."

"But I can't stay here for two weeks," I protested. "I have to continue on to Genoa tomorrow. I must find Doctor Moro as soon as possible so he can turn me into a real boy. I'm running down day by day; every day is precious to me."

"I don't have the slightest idea what you're babbling about," said the leader, "but you have no say in the matter. You can see that the rest of them would just as soon finish you off now. You should thank me that I'm not giving in to them."

He turned to the other three: "Take him to the town hall and throw him in a cell." To me he said, "If you're lucky, you'll have the cell all to yourself. It's quite small, but you'll find it homey."

With those words the leader turned and walked out of the room. The stout man and the bearded man each gripped an arm and carried me out, my feet kicking vainly in the air. The pimply man stuffed my hat, my blanket, and Gregorio's empty cage in my knapsack and followed behind. Gregorio had managed to hop on my shoulder during the hubbub, and hunched there unnoticed as the men bore me away.

I was still kicking and shouting protests when we reached the town hall. The posse told the jailer that I was probably a horse thief who would be hanged in a month, but that they were obliged to hold me until the day Signor Godoti was to return home, just in case I might be telling the truth— not that they expected him to return, of course.

"Just look at his criminal features, Cornelio!" exclaimed the pimply man. "You can tell from his face that he's a sub-human creature—see how hard he looks." The jailer looked at me and shook his head. Without a word, he took a worn brass key from a hook on the wall and gestured for the men to follow him. They marched me down a gray corridor towards a reddish light shining weakly out of the darkness. As we neared the end of the corridor, I saw that the light shone from a pine knot smoldering in a brazier standing by a door in the end wall.

The jailer opened the door. I peered inside and saw an inky void—my home for the next two weeks. The jailer jerked his head toward the dark opening; my captors pushed me inside and slammed the door. In utter blackness, I heard the key throw the bolt; I heard retreating footsteps and fading laughter; then I heard nothing at all. I banged on the hard iron with my wooden fists, but no one responded, and the stone walls swallowed up the echoes of my blows. I sat down on the stone floor and hung my head between my knees in despair.

After a few minutes Gregorio spoke. "It's not as bad as it seems, Pinocchio. Signor Godoti will return home in two weeks and put everything right; then we'll be on our way again. You still have almost half a year before you run down; that's enough time."

I stood up and walked around the cell. The chocolate within ceased to churn; the frantic beating of my mechanical heart returned to the measured pace Giuseppe had set. I knew my friend was right. I was no longer afraid, but I was very angry. I stood accused of a crime I didn't commit. Now, my conscience was never troubled when I escaped punishment for the bad things I did, but to be accused of one wicked deed that I didn't do filled me with a great sense of injustice and betrayal. The chocolate bubbled up again, not in fear but in indignation. How could God allow this to happen to me? Even though the merchant would return soon and confirm my innocence, I was angry at God for letting me get into this mess. It never occurred to me that God might have put me in that cell for a purpose.

As my eyes grew accustomed to the darkness, I discovered that the cell was not really pitch black at all. It had a small barred window facing south. I could see the full moon above the Appenines; it was the same view I had enjoyed from my room in the guest house. By the time the moon was new Signor Godoti would return and this meaningless delay would be over.

I passed the next fourteen days impatiently. I continued to muse on the great injustice of it all. Gregorio tried once or twice to bring me round to a better frame of mind, but I replied so savagely that he hopped off in disgust to a corner of the cell and spoke only when spoken to, which was seldom.

I awoke in a much better mood on the fifteenth day. "Today Signor Godoti is due home, Gregorio! Finally the truth will come out and we'll be out of here and on the road again. I apologize for my ugly mood these two weeks; I haven't been human."

"No, you've been all too human, Pinocchio; I was a human once, I know these things. But let's not discuss that," he added hastily. "The sooner we're out of here, the better."

The sun climbed high in the southern sky as the minutes became hours, then began its ride to the western horizon. My mood turned foul again. Where was the jailer? Why hadn't he come to release me with apologies? When he brought my evening meal—my fifteenth bowl of watery rutabaga soup—I anxiously asked him about Signor Godoti.

"I expect you know more about his whereabouts than we do," replied the jailer. "It's no use your trying to keep up appearances like this. Godoti hasn't returned, and he won't return, him lying dead where you left him. The magistrate will be here in a week; we all can count on *his* timely appearance. Then you won't have any more waiting to do; justice will be timely, too."

"Godoti must have stayed an extra day somewhere; no doubt business was very good up north," I answered, panicky; but the jailer had already closed the door and gone. I turned to Gregorio. "Godoti has been delayed, but he'll be here tomorrow; surely he'll come tomorrow."

"Of course," my friend agreed in an uncertain voice, "he's bound to arrive tomorrow. Business delayed him, or maybe another thunderstorm over the Po. He'll be here tomorrow."

But Godoti did not come the next day, nor the day after that. By the third day of the new moon Gregorio and I had abandoned all pretence of hope. For six days I couldn't eat or sleep, certain now that he wouldn't come at all.

"Signor Godoti has been waylaid and murdered by the bandit Pietraviva, Gregorio, that's what's happened. How could the Lord let this happen to us?"

The door of the cell opened before Gregorio could reply. The jailer stood there with a smile on his face.

"I am here to announce that Signor Godoti has arrived back in town. We were overjoyed to see him, for we were convinced that you had murdered our friend. We told him all about you."

"Wonderful!" I cried. "Now we can go!"

"Go?" said the jailer. "Signor Godoti told us that you stole his horse while he was napping under a tree. He awoke as you were riding away. He gave us a very accurate description of the thief, a description that matches you perfectly. He has taken Clover home now. He'll come back tomorrow to testify before the magistrate. I would guess that since you didn't kill Signor Godoti you will get off with five years in prison."

The jailer gave a short, harsh laugh and slammed the door. I turned to Gregorio in misery, confusion, and dread.

Chapter 23

The jailer's laughter faded away down the corridor. Gregorio spoke first. "Snap out of it, Pinocchio. We've got to think of a way out of here."

We put our heads together but got nowhere: we were trying to think but nothing was happening. All we could see were the obstacles. Our flight to freedom was blocked by three solid oaken doors: the cell door, the corridor door, and the door to the street. The tiny window that taunted me with a glimpse of light and freedom was fitted with cold iron bars. Even if I could wriggle (somehow) through the bars and gain the windowsill, I would be stuck thirty feet above the piazza, exposed to the eyes of the whole city. The only way down from there was to jump—a quick way to turn myself to splinters. Luck and wit had got us out of a half-dozen tight spots so far, but now we had run out of both.

I paced the floor, scuffing my shoes and not caring. Five years! Five months would have been a death sentence. My heart was as heavy and cold as the stone walls of the prison. I stared out the window with tears in my eyes. Just over those mountains lay Genoa and my hope of becoming a real boy. Gregorio might make it there without me; he could fly out the window whenever he wanted. My own hopes were dead.

"Pinocchio," Gregorio said softly, "you must not despair. You *do* have one hope left. It would take a miracle to deliver you, so you must turn to God."

I bowed my head. "Lord God of my father Gepetto, I confess that I have no other hope left but you. I prayed to you before and you led me to Gregorio and saved us both from that wicked Ladrone. Please save us again. I didn't keep my first promise to serve and obey you always, but I have learned my lesson now. If you can free me from this prison—I mean, if you *will* free me from this prison—please do. This time I'll be so good that I'll make up for all the bad things I've done."

"No you won't," said a soft voice behind me, a voice I knew. I turned and saw her—Gabriela!

"It's the angel!" squeaked Gregorio. In the dim light I couldn't tell if the satin-robed, dark-haired figure standing there was the girl I loved or the angel Gregorio believed her to be.

"You can't make up for all the bad things you've done," she continued. "The price of forgiveness is more than you could pay. Besides, you'll go on to do even worse things than you've done. But God has sent me with good news for you. Giuseppe's son, Giovanni, is searching for you. When he finds you he will tell you how you can both become real boys."

"But tomorrow they'll sentence me to prison, probably for five years," I exclaimed. "They'll lock me away me in a cell deeper and darker than this one. Giovanni will never find me. The woodcarver's son may have a plan to transform a living boy of wood into a living boy of flesh and blood, but he'll have to do more than that. In five months some guard will find a motionless dummy curled up on the floor of my cell—my poor remains after I've run down. Can Giovanni raise the dead?"

"No," Gabriela replied, "and he won't need to, for I've been sent to free you from this jail." With those words the angel turned and touched the oaken door with her shepherd's staff. The door twisted off its hinges and fell outward, making a terrible crash as it hit the floor. "Follow me," Gabriela said, "and don't worry about the noise. I've already put the jailer to sleep."

I scooped up my belongings, Gregorio hopped on my hat, and we trotted down the corridor after our angel. When she reached the second door she touched it with her staff and it too fell open; I was sure the rattle must have roused the whole city. Gabriela walked boldly into the jailer's office while I cautiously peeked around the edge of the door. The jailer was snoring softly. Gabriela searched through his strong box until she found a heavy iron key. She smiled with satisfaction and motioned for us to follow. We left the office and continued down the corridor to the outer door. This time she used the key—no need to send it crashing into the piazza and sound the alarm.

"Where do we go from here?" I asked her. "Am I to return to the village and await Giovanni?"

"Take any road you wish; Giovanni will find you." Gabriela paused, then continued: "I should tell you that your father,

Gepetto, also has left the village to search for you. He said he would look first in Genoa, then in Rome."

"Father! What worry and pain I've caused him! Gregorio, we must continue on to Genoa and look for Father. After we find him we'll all return home and wait for Giovanni." I started down the steps, then turned back to thank Gabriela. She had vanished.

It was about four in the afternoon. I looked out on the piazza from the middle of the steps.

People were crossing the square in all directions, each concerned with his own affairs. No one showed any interest in me.

I descended to the cobbled pavement and casually walked across the square to the mouth of a narrow street. Entering the street, I quickened my pace. I walked briskly through one twisting street after another, going as fast as I could without drawing attention to myself. When I reached the edge of the city, I found no one else on the road; then I took to my heels. The authorities would discover my escape soon enough.

When I had run a mile, I turned and looked back towards Novi. The distant city resembled a frosted layer cake, its limestone walls gleaming white in the afternoon sun. All was still. I saw no commotion around the gate and heard no alarm. I was not yet missed.

My chest was pounding and my lungs burned. I slowed to a walk. As my breath returned, Gregorio and I began to talk.

"What do you think, Gregorio? Was it the angel Gabriele or the girl Gabriela who visited us?"

"Our rescuer had to be an angel, Pinocchio. Girls don't pass through stone walls or appear and disappear with a snap of the fingers. I never knew Gabriela well, but I know that she is a real girl, not a spirit."

"Oh, I agree that she's a flesh-and-blood girl, Gregorio; but don't you think the Lord enables people to do miracles, too? Doesn't He send them on missions of mercy? Our miraculous messenger knew all about what was happening in the village, like one who lived there. And she looked just like Gabriela. I would have expected an angel to look more fearsome, more awe-inspiring, if you know what I mean."

"Our rescuer was awe-inspiring to me, Pinocchio. She knocked those doors down with a mere touch of her staff. The deeds, not the appearance, have convinced me. Didn't you tell me that angels visited Father Abramo before they destroyed Sodoma and Gomorra? They were angels, but they looked just like men. We were rescued by an angel for sure."

We might have argued back and forth all the way to Genoa, but at that moment a long howl stopped me in my tracks. A hound! I wheeled around and looked back down the road. I was too far away to see the city anymore, but a small cloud of dust was rising behind me where the road shrank to a point. They were coming after me, with dogs!

I looked around in panic. We were still in the cultivated plain, a good five miles from the woods that ran down from the foothills. I could plunge into a wheat field and cower in the ripening grain, but the dogs would sniff me out without fail. Then my desperate eyes fell on a creek winding lazily through the field on my right. Perfect! The dogs couldn't follow my scent in the water. I would wade up the creek till I threw them off my scent.

I ran till I reached a culvert where the muddy water glided under the road and jumped into the ditch without hesitation. The creek received the water that drained from the fields and farms round about and stank like manure, but it was only waist deep. The green-brown water flowed so slowly that I could barely sense its motion, but over time it had carved a winding gully five feet below the level of the field. No one could see me from above.

As I made my way up the sluggish creek I came upon one small ditch after another emptying into the main watercourse. Even if my pursuers waded up the gully after me they wouldn't know which way to turn. I was safe for the moment.

I slogged on upstream till daylight faded and the sky began to turn indigo. Night was falling fast. I was exhausted; I had to find a place to rest before it got too dark to go safely. Sinking my fingers into the top of the bank, I pulled my body out of the muck, but could not get a foothold in the damp, crumbly earth. I straightened my arms, locked my elbows, and began to swing my legs back and forth until I was almost horizontal. With one last swing I cleared the top, my wooden body rattling as it came down on the edge of the bank.

Standing up, I found myself in a wheat field. I had no idea how far I had come or where I was, for the standing grain hemmed me in on all sides. I began to make my way through the tall wheat,

Even if my pursuers waded up the gully after me they wouldn't know which way to turn. I was safe for the moment.

keeping the low, red sun on my right hand. Shallow ditches cut across my path on their way to the creek. I tripped and fell several times in my haste to get as far as possible before I had to stop for the night.

"Pinocchio, watch where you're going!" my friend exclaimed. "If you break a leg you're done for."

I slowed my pace but pushed on, using my arms like a swimmer to force my way through the tall wheat. The sun sank too soon and the flat countryside began to disappear in dusky shadows. I bent over till my nose almost touched the ground as I strained to make out those perilous ditches. Eyes fixed on the earth beneath my feet, I didn't see the robbers' camp until I stepped out of the wheat and stumbled into a man sitting hunched over a campfire.

Chapter 24

I flew over the man and landed spread-eagled in a ploughed furrow—fortunately, I didn't land in the fire. When I lifted my face from the dirt I found myself nose to nose with Pietraviva himself, the dread bandit chief who had all of Novi talking.

There was no mistaking that grim face for a wandering Gypsy or a lesser member of the robber band. Above a scowling mouth and drooping mustache two black eyes stared into mine from dark, sunken sockets. They were brave, intelligent eyes, eyes to compel obedience with a single glance. Now they glittered feverishly. Small crimson drops stood on the man's brow—not blood, but sweat reflecting the dull red campfire. Black locks flecked with gray and matted with more sweat clung to his brow. I realized then that Pietraviva's face was not scowling with anger, but twisting with pain.

I had stumbled into the robbers' camp at a time of crisis. Hundreds of carabinieri were scouring the whole country from the mountains to the Po in search of Pietraviva's band. The robbers were trying to get back to the safety of their mountain lair. They had been in this kind of spot before; it was one of the usual hazards of their trade. But this time their capo, or head, was sick or injured. All this I saw in the few seconds before Pietraviva spoke.

"I don't know who you are or how you came here, boy; but in less than a minute I am going to have Tomasso break your spine in three places and throw you in the nearest ditch." The capo gestured towards a mountain of muscle standing above me, a heavy-browed brute with a cruel, stupid smile. The man's fingers twitched at the capo's words. "Can you suggest some reason I should not do this?"

I smiled my broadest, warmest, friendliest smile and began to speak lies for my life.

"Signor Pietraviva, I presume? Like you, I'm on the run from the police. I was hoping to find you; I'd like to join your band. Perhaps you've lost a man or two on this raid and need a replacement? I offer my service. I may not be big or strong but I do know how to get out of a tight spot: just today I escaped from the Novi jail."

Pietraviva turned to one of his men. "Bartolomeo, you returned from Novi this evening. Did you hear anything about a jail break?"

"As a matter of fact, I did, capo. The citizens were forming a posse to look for a lad who had escaped just an hour earlier, a day before he was to be sentenced for his crime."

"Why were you in jail? What did you do?" the capo asked with effort.

Words came easily to me now; as I spoke I could feel the chocolate stirring inside. At the time I thought that strange, for I didn't think I was doing anything wrong; I was only telling a few white lies to save my skin.

"They arrested me for stealing a merchant's horse on the road between Alessandria and Novi. Unfortunately, I didn't know the man was from Novi. While passing through town, his friends recognized the horse and had me arrested."

"We don't need another thief. Tomasso, he's yours."

"Wait!" I cried quickly. "You do need a horse thief. I can see you've been injured. You're suffering great pain; you can't walk, much less fight. If you're going to get away from here you'll have to find a mount, and you'll have to do it before morning light. The carabinieri have dogs; they're sure to find you tomorrow if you're still here. Then you'll die in agony in this miserable field.

"Put me to the test," I hurried on. "I know where the horse is. Send Tomasso with me and I'll steal it a second time and bring it here. If I do that, will you give me safe passage to Genoa? I've got to get to Genoa; my life, too, is at stake. I need you as much as you need me. The carabinieri are watching the highway and the pass over the mountains. I don't know this country; they're bound to catch me if I go on alone. You know secret ways over the mountains; you can get me to Genoa safely. Make a deal with me: I bring you a horse; you lead me to Genoa."

"So, you don't really want to join my band after all. Well, that doesn't matter. You're shrewd, boy; you've put your finger right on my dilemma." The capo narrowed his eyes and gave me a half smile: "But are you shrewd enough, boy? How do you know I won't kill you after you've kept your end of the bargain?"

"You are the great Pietraviva, a capo of men. There may be no honor among common thieves, but a capo keeps his sworn word."

"You're doubly shrewd, boy; you know that honor means more to a man like me than life itself. Enough! We have a deal. I'll send Andrea with you instead of Tomasso. Tomasso is very disappointed that I didn't let him fold your spine in half. I have doubts about Tomasso; I'm afraid you might meet with an accident coming back from Novi." The other robbers—there were about a dozen, as well as I could make out by the campfire—laughed at this. Tomasso laughed, too, but kept clenching and unclenching his fingers.

The robber chief ordered Andrea to tie one end of a rope around my waist and the other around himself.

"Just in case our young friend is tempted to wander off on his own, Andrea, we'll ensure that he remains your inseparable companion on this caper. By the way, boy, what's your name and where are you from?"

"My name is Pinocchio, capo, and I'm from a small, nameless village in the foothills of the Alps."

Pietraviva received this information without comment and sent us off. Andrea led the way by the light of the waning moon, which had now risen. We did not speak. Gregorio, who had been silent most of the evening, began to talk to me.

"If you want my opinion, Pinocchio, you made a mistake in lying and trying to talk your way out of trouble."

"What do you mean, lying? I was in jail for stealing a horse, and I did break out. If I hadn't come up with that story fast Tomasso would be picking splinters out of his fingers now, splinters that used to be me. Surely it's all right to lie to save your own neck."

"Have you no faith in the Lord? He would have sent that angel to rescue us again, I'm sure of it. Your nose is an inch longer, I can tell you that. What other proof do you need that you chose the easier but worse path out of trouble? Why didn't you pray?"

"I thought of that, but I was afraid the Lord would save us at the cost of our property. Clover is ours and I'm going to try to get her back. I'll pray if my scheme falls through."

"Doesn't the Bible say something about not loving the world or the things in it? Something about gaining the world and losing your life?"

"Yes, it does; and I'll give up my horse and my money if it comes to that. But I don't see why it has to come to that. Why can't I be a good Christian and be well-off as well?"

Gregorio and I were well launched into an argument about the ways of God again. I enjoyed these arguments, all the more so because the aroma of chocolate came drifting up from deep inside

The other robbers—there were about a dozen, as well as I could make out by the campfire—laughed at this. Tomasso laughed too, but kept clenching and unclenching his fingers.

me when I really got into them. I wasn't seeking the truth in all my disputes with Gregorio; I just liked the give and take.

Our argument ended when I caught up with Andrea. We were following a country lane, and Andrea had stopped where it entered the highway. A quarter-mile ahead the highway disappeared into a high arch in the city wall.

"Well, Pinocchio," Andrea said, "the gate is shut for the night. How does our master horse thief propose to get into the city? The merchant does live in town, doesn't he?"

"I have no idea where he lives, Andrea." The fellow looked astonished, so I quickly continued: "Although I don't know where Signor Godoti lives, and the gate is shut and barred, I have a plan for getting into the city and finding the merchant's house." I told him my plan. My companion grinned and slapped me on the back. "Maybe you are a master thief after all," he said. "I would never have thought of that, but I do believe it will work. Let's do it."

Andrea walked boldly up to the gate and pounded on the heavy planking until the guard appeared in the gatehouse window.

"Who are you, and what do you think you're doing, banging on the gate at this hour? You should know that the gate won't be opened till sunrise."

"My name is Andrea Piccolo. I keep a small farm six miles south of here. I found this lad asleep in my hayloft this evening. I heard that a boy of his general description escaped from jail this afternoon. Would you recognize him?"

"Not I," said the guard. "The boy you mention was jailed at city hall. I'm stuck out here on the gate every night and never see the prisoners there."

"Well, I could take him to jail and let the guard there tell me if I've caught a real thief or just a tramp, but I'm afraid I'd just get them mad if I woke them up and it was a false alarm. Is there someone else in town who could identify him first? How about the merchant whose horse he stole?"

"That would be Signor Godoti. Yes, take your prisoner by Godoti's house and let the old miser have a look at him. It doesn't matter if you rouse him out of bed. Even if he gets mad he can't make trouble for you. Take the third turn to the right after you enter the gate and go to the end of the street. Godoti lives in the second house from the end on the left."

"Thanks for your help. If there's a reward I'll bring you back a bottle of wine to keep you warm on your watch."

With that exchange of words the guard unlocked the gate and let in Andrea and me. I walked slowly, with bowed head; I knew how to play the part of a crook who knew the jig was up.

As soon as we were out of sight of the gatehouse Andrea grinned and slapped me on the shoulder again.

"That was really clever, Master Pinocchio." Then he paused, and his smile disappeared. "Do you also have a plan to steal the horse without waking up the town? And how about getting out of town with the horse?

"Leave it to me," I assured him.

When we reached Godoti's house we stopped in the shadows. I told Andrea I had to think a bit. Actually, the job was now in Gregorio's hands, but I didn't want Andrea to know about Gregorio. I pretended to work out a plan in my head while Gregorio jumped down and went to look over Godoti's place. Andrea took no notice of the cricket that hopped across the street in front of us.

My friend returned sooner than I expected. "We're in luck, Pinocchio," he squeaked. "Clover is in a stable behind the house, through that gate in the wall there. I talked to her; she's more than ready to come with us."

I turned to Andrea. "Untie me, please. I've figured out where the horse must be. Don't worry about me escaping; I'm going through that gate over there and I have to come out the same way. Besides, I need the rope for the horse."

Andrea saw that I spoke the truth so he untied me, coiled up the rope, and gave it to me. I looked both ways and saw that the street was deserted. I quickly crossed over and disappeared through the gate.

Less than a minute passed before I returned leading Clover. Andrea broke into his wide grin again (revealing two missing teeth) and gave a silent thumbs up sign.

You may be wondering how we planned to get out of Novi with Clover. Gates that keep robbers out can also keep them in! In fact, breaking out of the city was easier than breaking in. It was only ten o'clock in the evening and the trattorias were still open. Andrea bought a bottle of brandy and went to visit the guard at the gate while I waited with Clover in the shadows.

"It was him all right," crowed Andrea as he gave the guard the brandy. "That little thief is back behind bars where he belongs. The reward was generous so I brought you brandy instead of wine to show my appreciation for your help."

They drank a glass together; then Andrea rose to go. "I've decided to stay in town tonight. It's getting chilly, so I'll be leaving now. I want to find a room in a nice, warm trattoria. Good night, friend. I hope the brandy keeps you warm during your watch."

Andrea joined me in the shadows and we watched the guard drink the brandy, one glass after another, until he finished the whole bottle. In less than an hour he was sprawled across the tiny table in the guardhouse, sound asleep. I tiptoed into the stone cubicle and softly removed the key ring from his belt. I might just as well have announced my entry with trumpets blaring; the slumbering sentinel wouldn't have noticed. I unlocked the gate and opened it so Andrea could lead Clover out, then I placed the keys on the table in front of the sleeping guard's nose. I hoped he would wake up before his relief came at dawn, see the keys, and lock the gate. He was a good fellow; I didn't care to see him fired from his job for leaving the gate unlocked. If he locked the gate and kept his mouth shut Clover's disappearance would remain a mystery.

We shut the gate and made our way back to the robbers' camp. I had kept my end of the bargain; I trusted that Pietraviva would keep his and bring me safely to Genoa.

Chapter 25

Pietraviva was delighted to see us return before midnight with the promised horse. Andrea sang my praises.

"Capo, the boy's a genius! I was alarmed when he told me he didn't know where the horse was to be found. But he came up with a plan that got us past the guard at the gate, led us right to the horse, and got us out of town again. I didn't think we could ever get into town without being stopped, much less find a horse and return; but this boy, a mere lad, knew just what to do." The chocolate bubbled happily within me; its fumes swelled my pride like hot air swells a balloon.

Pietraviva spoke: "Excellent, lad! You kept your end of the bargain; now you shall see that there is honor among thieves. I will bring you safely to Genoa."

And he did. I suppose it would take another book to tell you all that happened to Gregorio and me between the robbers' camp and Genoa. I'll tell you only that we encountered surprise, danger, and sure signs of the Lord's presence on our way up and over the Appenines and down to the sea. A journey of two days became an ordeal of two months; but on the fifteenth of September we said goodbye to Pietraviva in the hills above Genoa.

Clover decided to stay with Pietraviva. I sold her when she made it clear that she didn't want to go on. My insect friend retold his conversation with her.

"Clover, the city below is Genoa. We'll find the famous Doctor Moro there and he'll transform us into real human beings."

"Gregorio, I don't want to go any farther with you. I want to stay with Pietraviva and be his mount."

"But Clover! You have a chance to rise from horse to man! You set out with us in the hope of becoming a human being; how can you turn back now?"

"I've been thinking a lot about my future in the past weeks. The world is full of many men, almost all of them common and ordinary. If Doctor Moro turns me into a man or a woman I'm certain to be one of the herd. No one will know me or remember me after I die. But if I stay with Pietraviva, I'll be the mount of the most famous bandit in Italy. Men still praise Alessandro Magno, who conquered the world, and they still remember his horse, Bucefalo. I want to be famous like Bucefalo; I want men to remember my name after I'm gone."

"Do you realize what you're doing?" Gregorio asked. "You're trading away the opportunity to be made in the image of God for fame. God made man in His image. How can you be satisfied being a horse when you could be made over in God's image?"

"The men I've seen don't show me much of God," Clover snorted. "I can't believe they reflect His image."

"Not now," answered Gregorio. "When Adamo sinned, that image was marred and men became like beasts—look at me for proof of that! But Gepetto told me God recreates men in His image again through Christ. As for myself, I can hardly believe He wants to recreate me in His image—I've seen my sin Clover, and I am vile. Yet I have a little hope that it might be true, and I know that this hope is only for human beings. It's not for crickets or horses. It's worth taking a chance, Clover, for if you choose to remain a horse you will surely die some day. So what if men remember you as the mount of the great capo Pietraviva? You'll never know; you'll be nothing. There's nothing beyond this life for animals. Come with us, Clover!"

"Honestly, Gregorio, I don't believe Doctor Moro or anyone else can make me a human being. I accept my fate: someday I'll die and pass into nothingness. The best thing for an animal is to enjoy all the fame and pleasure this life offers. Being Pietraviva's own saddle horse offers a lot. I'll be well cared for and I'll share in the cheers of the peasants as he rides among them, thumbing his nose at carabinieri and rich merchants like Godoti."

Clover couldn't be persuaded, so with tears in my eyes I sold her to Pietraviva. Clover was not a prime specimen of horseflesh, but she had carried the robber chief loyally and gently over the mountains, and he had grown fond of her. Pietraviva and I haggled a bit and agreed on a fair price. He handed me the money; I gave him Clover's reins. Pietraviva and I embraced; I patted Clover on the muzzle, and turned away to hide my tears. When I looked back I saw horse and rider disappearing into a thicket of laurel and scrub oak—no reason to risk being seen on the road. I turned and started downhill towards the city. I never saw either of them again.

The steep road switchbacked down a narrow, dry ravine. Halfway down the hill a spring gurgled out of a mossy cleft in the rock and trickled down a ditch that ran beside the road. I stopped to drink and gaze at the sight before me. Villas and estates straddled the hills on either side of the ravine all the way down to the narrow plain where the great city, a mass of yellow brick, lay crowded between the hills and the sea.

Genoa! I forgot all about Clover and my hardships as I started briskly down the road again. My heart was light and full of hope. I had to share my excitement with Gregorio.

"That's Genoa down there, Gregorio! I have another two or three months left before my spring runs down. We're sure to find Father before then, and Giovanni, too, or maybe Doctor Moro."

"Whom do you want to take a chance on, Pinocchio, Giovanni or the Doctor?" asked Gregorio.

"The one we find first," I replied. "I don't believe there's only one way to become a real boy. God would not be so narrow as to have only one way, would He?"

"I don't know," Gregorio answered thoughtfully. "Most of the time I don't believe God intends to make me a real boy again, so one way would be enough for me. I don't think we should be telling God how He ought to do things. I once heard a priest read the Scripture where the Savior says that the way to eternal life is narrow while the way to destruction is broad. I remember that sermon because my father swore never to go back to church after that. He thought the priest was too narrow-minded; but I knew it was the Lord's word, not the priest's. If the Lord has only one way for us to become real boys and be saved, we'd do well to find it rather than haggle about narrowness."

"I don't see any harm in giving Doctor Moro a try if we find him first," I replied. "If he can turn us into real boys, it will save Giovanni the trouble. If he can't, we'll look for Giovanni.

"But more important than finding Doctor Moro or Giovanni is finding Father. How I miss him!"

Thinking of Father, I fell silent. Somewhere in the city below a middle-aged man was trudging through the streets and lanes looking for his wooden son. Very soon I would be there, too, searching the sea of passing faces for Father's anxious face as I wandered through that maze of brick and stone. How could we expect to find each other? And what about Doctor Moro—where would I look for him? How could Giovanni find me? The city was so big, so strange. My quest seemed hopeless. The more I thought about it, the more confused and depressed I became.

Gregorio and I had been together so long that he knew me as well as I knew myself. I hadn't spoken a word or breathed a sigh, but he knew I was on the edge of despair and he knew why.

"It's not at all as impossible as it appears, Pinocchio," he chirped bravely. "We're not in this alone. You found me after Ladrone kidnapped me; that was a more hopeless situation than the present one. The Lord brought you to me by strange and unexpected means. He'll do the same now."

Good old Gregorio! His words cleared away my gloomy fog like the morning breeze puts nighttime mist to flight. I knew what we had to do first. Kneeling right there beside the road, I prayed once more.

"Lord God of my father," I pleaded, "I come to you again because I have no other hope. The city is so big and I am so small. Please lead me to Father. You know how I want to become a real boy, a flesh-and-blood son for him. Please send Giovanni to tell me how to become a real boy, or lead me to Doctor Moro so that he can do it, if there is a Doctor Moro. And thank you for delivering me from jail, for saving us from Ladrone, and for everything else you've done. I wish, Lord, that I remembered to be grateful all the time, not just when I'm in trouble; but I'm grateful now. And please keep me out of more trouble."

"Amen," squeaked my friend when I finished. "Well, Pinocchio, are you ready now to enter Genoa?" he asked. Lifting my head, I saw that we had paused just outside the city wall. I was so absorbed in my thoughts that I hadn't noticed how far we had come. The graceful arch of the Soprano Gate rose like a pair of praying hands above me. Somewhere inside awaited Father, Doctor Moro, Giovanni, and hope for Gregorio and me.

"Amen," squeaked my friend when I finished. "Well, Pinocchio, are you ready now to enter Genoa?" he asked.

Chapter 26

Gregorio and I scoured Genoa for a week without success. The only fruit of our daily explorations was that we got to know the city well. We visited the great palaces, piazzas, and churches of the city they call La Superba; we also saw the seamy side of Genoa, the wharves and taverns and slums. But we didn't find Father. There had to be some clue to put us on his trail—but what was it?

On the eighth day, as we were pushing through crowded streets towards the waterfront, it came to me all at once.

"What have I been thinking?" I exclaimed to my friend. "You would think I had sawdust for brains! Father doesn't know anyone in Genoa and he doesn't have the money to stay in an inn while searching for me. He would lodge with the Waldensian barbe. Gregorio, we've got to find the Waldensian church."

"Of course; what fools we've been!" agreed my companion, slapping his hard forehead with a jointed leg. "Let's ask the good Genoese where the Waldenses meet for worship." I began to ask one passerby after another how to get to the Waldensian church; but everyone I questioned was Catholic and had no idea who the Waldenses were, much less where their church might be. After three hours, I was almost convinced that there were no Waldenses in Genoa. Then, to my great joy, I found a man who was himself a Waldense.

He introduced himself as Brother Mateo and insisted on taking me to the church and introducing me to the barbe personally. "It's God's providence that you stopped me, Brother, for there are only a few of us in Genoa. Our church is near the port, just a block from the Palazzo di San Giorgio."

The minister, Barbe Marco, greeted me with an abbraccio and offered me coffee and a biscotto, which I shared with Gregorio—well, to be perfectly honest, I let him eat the crumbs. When I had explained my quest, Barbe Marco threw up his hands.

"Ah, young man, you're too late! Brother Gepetto came here, just as you guessed. He lodged with me for a week while he searched the city for you. But he left Genoa a month ago after hearing a rumor that his son, Pinocchio, was looking for a certain Doctor Moro."

The minister, Barbe Marco, greeted me with an abbraccio and offered me coffee and a biscotto, which I shared with Gregorio—well, to be perfectly honest, I let him eat the crumbs. When I had explained my quest, Barbe Marco threw up his hands.

"That's true!" I exclaimed. "Were you able to direct him to Doctor Moro? Where does Doctor Moro live? How can I get there?" I was excited: if Father was with Doctor Moro I would find the one when I found the other!

"Doctor Moro doesn't live in Genoa, though he visits now and again. People say he's a famous scientist; I wouldn't know. They say he lives on an island off Portofino, a fishing village just this side of Rapallo. As to getting there, I hope you can find a boat in Portofino. No one from Genoa will take you there. Doctor Moro has an evil reputation in this city and people are afraid of him."

"Why is that?" I asked.

"They say he conducts unnatural experiments; I wouldn't know. Some think he's in league with the devil; that I doubt. But I've seen some of his patients after he operated on them, and they didn't look human."

"Operated on them? Is Doctor Moro a scientist or a surgeon?" I inquired.

"Both. He does experimental surgery." Barbe Marco hesitated, then continued: "Little Brother, your father told me why you are looking for Doctor Moro. He also told me that Giovanni is looking for you. I urge you, wait for Giovanni! I know Brother Giuseppe and his son; I am confident that Giovanni knows how you and your cricket can become real boys."

"I would wait for him," I answered, "but I must find Father. Don't worry about me being taken in by Doctor Moro. If he's a quack doctor I'll know it right away. I've suffered too much from rogues to be fooled again."

I said goodbye to Barbe Marco and left as soon as good manners would permit. We went straight to the market, where we found a fisherman starting back to Portofino after selling his morning catch. He agreed to let us ride with him for two lire. It was only twelve miles to Portofino, and the wagon stank of fish, but I had been walking every day for two months. I was sick and tired of walking.

As the wagon rumbled south along the coastal road, Gregorio and I began to talk. He was a little nervous.

"Pinocchio, I think Barbe Marco was right. After we find your father we should all return home and wait for Giovanni. Let's just forget about Doctor Moro."

"Of course, friend, I agree entirely!" I said reassuringly. And for the moment, I really did agree. It was only when my plans fell apart that my good intentions crumbled with them, as you shall see.

We reached Portofino while the sun was still hot and high in the sky. The fisherman left us in the center of the village, by the sea wall. A dozen brightly-painted fishing boats lay side by side on the beach below the wall; a trattoria looked out on the sea from the other side of the road. Portofino was still a fishing village in those days, so small that it boasted only one public house. All the better for me, I thought. The proprietor would know everything that happened in the village; he would be able to direct me to Doctor Moro and Father.

Four deserted tables baked in the *mezzogiorno*, or midday sun that beat fiercely down on the terrace in front of the inn. Proprietor and customers would be inside now. I walked across the shimmering flagstones, pulled open the windowless door, and stepped out of the brilliant sunshine into the taproom.

The inside of the inn was as dark as a cave. I paused inside the door until my eyes got used to the dimness. Looking around, I saw three men at the table nearest to me. Two of them were thick-browed, hairy brutes wearing bandanas and coarse blue smocks; they appeared to be fishermen. The third man looked out of place in their company. He wore a white shirt and necktie, dress trousers with suspenders, and a frock coat; a top hat lay on the table in front of him. Unlike his companions, he was clean-shaven and had fine features—a high forehead, a long, straight nose, and piercing black eyes.

The three men chatted in low, relaxed tones and took no notice of me. I wasn't interested in them either. No one else was present except the proprietor, who tried to look busy wiping the same dozen glasses again and again. I approached him, ordered a glass of the house wine, and began to talk.

"Signor, I have come to Portofino to find my father, who came here looking for me a month ago."

"Why would he be looking for you here a month ago?" the innkeeper asked with a bland smile. "You weren't here then."

"He thought I would come here in search of Doctor Moro. The Doctor does live near here, doesn't he?"

"Describe your father, young man; maybe he did pass through our little village. Not much happens here that I don't know about." The innkeeper didn't answer my question about Doctor Moro, but my concern was for Father so I let that pass.

"My father is about fifty years old; short and plump; with a mustache, hazel eyes, and a button nose; bald, except for a fringe of gray. He is always merry; at least, he was till I left home. He would have been asking about me—my name is Pinocchio."

The man stopped wiping the glasses and drew his breath in sharply. "Yes, I remember your father now. As you say, he was here a month ago asking about you. He stayed a week to build a raft—very skilled he was with hammer and saw, as I recall—and then sailed away into the gulf."

"A raft! Why would he do that?"

"He said he intended to sail to the island of Doctor Moro."

"Why didn't he hire one of the boats here?"

The innkeeper did not reply, but bent over and resumed wiping his glasses. I didn't press the question, for I already knew the answer. Like the Genoese, the gentlefolk of Portofino were afraid of Doctor Moro. I decided to try another approach. Pulling my purse from my pocket, I jingled it in front of the publican's nose.

"I have freshly-minted gold ducats here. If you know a fisherman brave enough to venture out to Doctor Moro's island, I'd like to hire him to help me search for my father. If Father has drifted onto some desert island, I must find him; and if he has fallen into Doctor Moro's clutches, I must rescue him. If he has perished in a storm, perhaps we can find his raft. I must know what has happened to my father."

"I can answer some of your questions, Signor," said a voice behind me. I turned around to see the well-dressed man by the door beckoning me to join him and his companions. I picked up my wine, still untasted, and walked over to their table.

"Your concern for your father is worthy of praise. Let me relieve some of your fears. First of all, there are no islands off this coast except Doctor Moro's island, so you may be sure your father is not marooned on some barren shore. As for shipwreck, it's true that an early autumn storm swept the gulf three weeks ago, but I'm confident your father didn't perish in it. The Gulf of Genoa is swarming with ships at all times. Even if he was thrown overboard and drowned—God forbid!— someone would have sighted the empty raft and reported it. No such report has been received. I believe your father and his raft were picked up after the storm by a merchant vessel outbound from Genoa. Rest assured, he will be brought back to Genoa after the ship has delivered its cargo in Marseilles or Livorno or Barcelona."

"But Father sailed for the island of Doctor Moro," I replied anxiously. "What if he reached it and is now a prisoner of that mad scientist?"

"I assure you, your father is not on the island of Doctor Moro. I am able to state that with absolute certainty. You see, I am Doctor Moro."

Chapter 27

My wooden jaw dropped to my chest and I sat there dumbstruck. Before I could recover my poise Gregorio sprang to the top hat and hopped up and down on it till the Doctor noticed him.

"Doctor, listen to me!" he squeaked. "That's right; it is I, the cricket, who am speaking to you. We've heard wonderful accounts of your work. Before we learned that my friend's father had come this way we were looking for you to discuss a very profitable business matter. You've relieved our minds about Signor Gepetto; now we can turn our attention to business once again. But we've also heard disturbing stories about you. Will you take us to your island so we can determine for ourselves which reports are true, the good or the bad? My wooden friend, Signor Pinocchio, will show you that we're not as poor as we look."

I caught on to Gregorio's scheme at once. I let the ducats cascade to the table, flashing and splashing like golden rain. The crewmen whistled and Doctor Moro's eyes widened.

"I'm always interested in talking business with men—er, beings—of means. I would be happy to do whatever I can to disprove any evil reports you have heard about me. The simple folk around here spread horrible rumors, all based on ignorance. I suppose my secrecy has spawned this regrettable gossip; I have not been anxious for the world to know the nature of my experiments until they are perfected.

"My assistants and I will be returning to the island as soon as we have bought our weekly supplies. I invite you to come there with us. Look around to your heart's content—you will have perfect freedom of movement. You'll see that I am but a seeker of scientific truth and that the aim of my research is to benefit all creatures. You'll also find that your father is not on my island. We can discuss business after you two have satisfied yourselves that I'm telling the truth."

We gladly took the Doctor up on his offer. In less than an hour, I found myself amidships in his sloop, sacks and boxes piled high around me, with Gregorio perched on the brim of my hat as usual. The graceful vessel sliced silently through the glassy water. I looked back at our wake of creamy foam rolling like a carpet towards Portofino. The village swiftly shrank to a point and vanished from sight altogether as we sailed out into the gulf. I turned and gazed at the open sea before us. The pale blue sky and the dark blue sea met on a straight, unbroken horizon. I couldn't see the island that lay somewhere ahead, but I knew it would come into view well before the sun began to descend into the sea.

"Gregorio!" I called to my friend. "Tell me what you meant about doing business with Doctor Moro. After counseling me to wait for Giovanni and to have nothing to do with the Doctor, you aren't thinking of bargaining with him to make us real boys, are you?"

"Actually, Pinocchio, that is what I was thinking about—but only for me," my friend said with some embarrassment. "Giovanni will tell you how to become a flesh-and-blood boy; the angel Gabriele himself told you that; but I haven't any faith that he can to restore me to the human race.

"Sometimes I think there is mercy for me, then I think about my disregard for the Lord all the years of my life and about all my sins and I just can't believe it.

"So, if Doctor Moro proves to be a truthful man, I would be willing to take a chance on him. If the Doctor could restore me to the form of a boy, the Lord might find me less loathsome; then He might be willing to make me a real boy."

"Gregorio, I am surprised—no, shocked. Do you think God's grace is limited? You think you're too foul at present for Him to look on you with pity; you hope by appearing more human to be somehow more deserving of mercy. Did you lose your brains when you became an insect? Grace and mercy are never deserved. Father says we can't know why God shows mercy on some lost souls and not on others, but we can be sure that it's not because some are more deserving than others, for all are unworthy."

"Do you really believe that, Pinocchio?" my friend snapped back. "Are you unworthy, too? The last time we talked about these things you told me you deserved to be turned into a real boy because you were really a very nice puppet. Do you now admit that you, too, need grace?"

I didn't answer my friend. Down deep, where the chocolate never ceased to bubble softly, I still felt I wasn't so bad. I admitted to myself that I wasn't perfect, but I hadn't the faintest idea how sweet, dark chocolate had soaked into every pore of my wooden self. I thought I was only a little sinner; I trusted that God was big enough to overlook my little failings and reward my many wonderful qualities.

Now Gregorio had caught me off guard. His question made me face up to the difference between what I believed about myself and what Father had taught me about grace. He had told me that everyone needs grace; no one deserves salvation. San Paolo had written that all have sinned and come short of God's glory; that there is none righteous, no, not one; that no one is saved except through God's free grace in Christ.

I knew it would take a power outside myself to make me a flesh-and-blood boy, but I couldn't accept that I was so utterly unworthy that I had no claim on God's power. Aha! What if Doctor Moro had the power to make me a real boy? I had plenty of money; I could pay him to do the job. If he succeeded, it would prove I wasn't so totally depraved that only God could save me. Then I would offer God my service as a real boy, and He would be pleased to accept such a fine boy as one of His own. I would be a credit to His cause; I would be His partner.

I finally answered my friend, though I didn't reply to his question. "I think it would be a good idea after all for us both to give Doctor Moro a try, provided that he's been telling us the truth about Father. As I said before, I'll turn to Giovanni if the Doctor cannot make me a real boy."

All at once we fell silent as the sloop came about and the island loomed suddenly ahead, seeming to burst from the sea like some spiny-backed sea dragon. A thin ribbon of level ground ran along the shore. Grassy slopes swept uphill from that wooded strip, tilting steeply as they climbed higher; finally they shot straight up, a sheer curtain of bare stone soaring a thousand feet towards heaven before running out of room to rise any higher. The line of cliffs was topped by a ragged ridge that ran across the island from one side to another, the naked spine of Doctor Moro's island.

The sloop made straight for the beach. On a knoll above our landing place stood a long, low villa walled in by wind-twisted pine trees. Before long I was helping Doctor Moro's men carry boxes and sacks up the path to the villa that was both home and laboratory for our host.

As I trudged behind the Doctor's two assistants, I looked at them closely for the first time. They were hairy brutes, as I had observed in the dark trattoria. Now, in the strong afternoon sun, I saw why they looked so beastly: they were dogs! Their tails had been chopped off, their teeth had been filed down, and their ears had been trimmed to human size, but their long torsos, short crooked legs, and jutting muzzles gave them away. Like Volpe and Gatto, they were animals made over in the image of man.

"Gregorio!" I whispered. "Those men are dogs!"

"I noticed it, too," he replied. "Remember, I have a hundred eyes. And just look at the servants who have come out to meet us!"

I looked up at the villa. A butler stood by the open door. He had a long straight face with fleshy drooping lips, and a ridge of coarse stringy hair ran back from his crown down his neck, disappearing under his collar. The butler was clearly a horse dressed up in striped pants and frock coat. The maid beside him wore the traditional black uniform with white apron and cap, but her tightly curled white hair betrayed her; dress as she would, she was still a sheep. The chef, who stood inside the door, had a round pink face with a snub nose, pointed ears, and squinty eyes—a pig if I ever saw one, though he did sport a white chef's hat and apron. A bearded gardener was working in the yard; he had to be a goat. All the servants had had their faces rearranged to make them appear human, but none of them would have fooled a baby.

The household staff relieved me of my burdens at the door and invited me in. I had to admit that they talked like humans, even though their looks betrayed their origin. Doctor Moro had already entered the villa and briefed the servants about our visit. The maid showed me to a pleasant room and informed me that supper would be at six. Until then, I was free to wander the island.

Gregorio and I set out at once to explore the villa. We began in the south wing. The south wing was like a hospital, containing an operating room, a laboratory, and a dozen private rooms. I examined all the rooms thoroughly. Some contained animals waiting for operations; others were occupied by heavily bandaged figures, animals who had already been under the surgeon's knife.

I talked with the patients to see if Father might be one of them, concealed by layers of gauze and drugged into helplessness. I quizzed them all: Had they seen a man answering to Father's

A bearded gardener was working in the yard; he had to be a goat. All the servants had had their faces rearranged to make them appear human, but none of them would have fooled a baby.

description? None of them had, and many had been on the island for more than a month. As I questioned them one by one they all told how happy they were that Doctor Moro had made them look human. They all realized the Doctor hadn't recreated them in perfect human form, but they were pleased to have taken a step in that direction.

In talking with the residents of the south wing, I learned a curious thing—most of them were donkeys! At the time, I concluded that donkeys, more than other animals, wanted to better their condition. I would later learn the horrible truth about Doctor Moro's donkeys—but let me tell that at its proper time.

We moved on to the center of the villa, Doctor Moro's personal living quarters. The Doctor graciously allowed us to search his rooms. We found nothing, so we proceeded to the north wing, which contained the laundry, kitchen, and dining room as well as the servants' bedrooms. The only door I didn't enter was a locked door in the wine cellar, but by that time I was convinced that Father was not on the island, nor ever had been.

Gregorio suggested that we go outside and walk around until dinner. We followed a rocky path up to the foot of the cliffs, then walked north along their base till we reached the sea. The rocky backbone of the island extended another quarter mile into the sea, making it impossible to walk the beach to the other side of the island, which had been our plan. We retraced our steps and walked to the south end of the island. Here, too, the central ridge jutted out into the sea. If we wanted to reach the other side of the island we would have to go by boat. I suggested that to Gregorio, but he saw no point in it.

"Pinocchio, your father isn't on this island; I don't think he ever came here."

I had to agree. No doubt Doctor Moro was right; Father had been picked up by an outbound ship after September's storm and would return to Genoa in a few weeks. Wouldn't it be wonderful if I could greet him at the dock as a real boy with Gregorio, also a real boy, at my side? Yes, we had business to discuss at supper with Doctor Moro.

Chapter 28

Dinner was over and the sun had set. We sat in Doctor Moro's study sipping hot chocolate. My, it was good! Strangely, I had never drunk hot chocolate in my life: water, wine, milk, and coffee, yes, but never chocolate. I can't begin to tell you how I enjoyed this new drink. It soaked into my arms and legs and filled them with blood and heat. The chocolate dissolved my last doubt and filled my heart with trust and good will towards our gracious host.

The Doctor sensed my openness and began to quiz me about our quest.

"Master Pinocchio, you said you might have some business to discuss if you found me honorable and trustworthy. Am I presuming too much if I ask you now what that business is?"

"No, my concerns have been relieved. I am ready to tell all. I told the innkeeper in Portofino that Father supposed I would come to Genoa in search of you. He was right. We have come many miles and braved many perils just to find you. As you see, I'm only a wooden boy. My friend, Gregorio, was once an ordinary boy, but he fell into his present state nearly a year ago. We both long to become real boys of flesh-and-blood. We sought you out because we were told you might be able to help us."

"Who told you that?" asked the Doctor, raising his eyebrows.

"Signor Volpe and Signor Gatto, whom you transformed from animals into something very much like human beings," I replied. "They spoke very highly of your abilities. They also said you would charge a good deal of money; but as you saw in Portofino, we have money and we're willing to spend it freely if you can make us over into real boys."

"Volpe and Gatto!" the Doctor murmured. "Yes, they were two of my most successful early cases. Of course, I've discovered much more since I operated on them. You would never know that some of my recent patients ever were animals."

"Doctor," I interrupted, "I think we know what you're trying to do here, but we would like you to explain your work to us in your own words."

"It would take too much time to explain it fully, Signor Pinocchio, and you don't have the scientific training to understand the details. But I can summarize my work briefly. My aim is to lift animals from their brutish state up to the level of human beings. Science tells us that man is not some spiritual being like God; he is simply the highest of the animals. It took man thousands, maybe millions, of generations to evolve from the lower animals. My noble goal is to turn animals into men in their own lifetime."

"And you are attempting to do this by means of surgery?" I asked.

"That is one line of research I am pursuing, yes. I call it the Method of Outer Change. Man is only an animal. He differs from other animals only in appearance. If I can make an animal look and behave like a man I have made it as human as it can be."

"Then you can't help me!" I cried in distress. "I already look human, but I'm not a real boy and I know it. What a creature looks like on the outside is nothing; it's what's inside that makes a being truly human."

"And you can't help me either!" squeaked Gregorio. "I don't look human now. Once I did, though now I am only an animal, just as you say. In an instant of hideous clarity I saw that I was a disgusting insect in God's sight. From that moment on, I have suffered in this repulsive body, a form proper to my true nature. If you can't change my inner self, you can't make me a real boy.

"Besides, even if I thought that restoring me to the form of a boy would make me a boy, I don't believe the most skillful surgeon could cut, tuck, and stitch my cuticle into human form. Foxes, cats, and donkeys, maybe, but not insects. I have six legs and a hundred eyes, not to mention wings and antennae. You would have to prune away half of me. I won't chance it."

"Hmm," the Doctor mused, "I see your point, Gregorio. I confess I've never attempted to remodel an insect. It would be a fascinating experiment, but it would be very risky, I admit that. As a naturalist, I don't accept your argument that the inner nature of a human being is different from an animal's, though I respect your views. Still, I must agree that for purely practical reasons you are not suitable subjects for the Method of Outer Change.

"But we can still do business," he hastily added, "for I have also been experimenting with the Method of Inner Change."

"What is that?" we asked together, puzzled.

"I believe there is a little bit of the human in all animals. The Method of Inner Change enlarges that bit of human nature until it overwhelms the lower nature and changes an animal into a man from the inside out. The more human the animal's nature becomes, the more human its form appears. When human nature has completely replaced the lower animal nature, the animal is a human being both inside and outside."

I shook my head. "Barbe Filippo says that God changes men by making them new, not by finding some little bit of good inside them and nourishing it. There isn't anything good to start with."

"Yes," chuckled the Doctor, "the Church teaches that. Of course, I don't believe man is so bad myself, although I respect your beliefs. But the Church doesn't teach anything about God changing animal nature, does it? God, if there is a God, has left it to science to discover how to elevate animal nature to human nature. And I have discovered the secret!" he whispered with triumph.

"What is it?" Gregorio asked excitedly. "What is your technique?"

"Proper diet. Man is what he eats. I have identified food that causes the human part of an animal to grow and the lower part of its nature to wither away. Also music and art. Not only what enters through the mouth, but also what enters through the ears and eyes, changes the inner self.

"Stay with me for a month. Eat and drink what I give you, listen to the music I choose for you, and gaze on the beautiful art I place before your eyes. Before the month is over you will both be true human beings, real boys. What do you say?" The Doctor paused, waiting for our reply.

"We'll give you our answer in the morning," I said, rising from my chair. "We've had a busy day. We'll sleep on your proposal and weigh it when our minds are fresh."

"Of course; take your time deciding. It could be a month before your father's ship returns to Genoa, so you need not rush. Good night, masters."

Doctor Moro left us in the study, our heads spinning with the fantastic ideas we had heard. Much as we wanted to talk them over then and there, we knew we were too tired to think clearly, so we went straight to our room and to bed.

The next morning Gregorio and I discussed the Doctor's Method of Inner Change before breakfast.

"I just don't feel right about it, Pinocchio," argued my friend. "I don't imagine it can do us any harm, but I find it hard to believe it can do us any good. Where does he get his ideas? Certainly not from the Bible!"

"He's no Christian, that's for sure," I agreed, "but he seems sincere; and there's no doubt he's very intelligent. Think how quickly he had answers for our objections."

"Oh yes, his tongue is quick enough," agreed Gregorio, with a wry smile.

I ignored Gregorio's sarcasm and continued: "You must agree that the Lord left some things unrevealed so that man might discover them for himself. We made this journey in the hope that Doctor Moro knew a way to turn animals into real human beings. Maybe he's on to something. I confess that the idea that I'm not totally bad, that I have a little bit of the human in me, does appeal to me."

"Yes, you've made that quite clear all along the way," Gregorio replied sharply. "Well, I suppose it won't hurt to give him a try. But I think we should abandon the treatment after two weeks if we detect no change within or without. After all, your time is drawing short. If Doctor Moro's method doesn't work you need time to find Giovanni; and we want to have some money left to get back home."

I saw the wisdom in Gregorio's suggestion. At breakfast we told the Doctor we would give his method a two-week trial. If we sensed we were becoming more human in that time, we would stay for a month, but if we observed no change we would leave. He looked a little disappointed, but agreed to give us two weeks of treatment for a ducat a day, each. I counted out twenty-eight gleaming coins into the Doctor's hand. His palm was moist and his eyes glittered as he received his fee.

Doctor Moro scurried away with the money, leaving us alone in the dining room. He returned shortly with the maid, who bore a tray with three dishes of food and two clean plates.

"We begin immediately," he said in a businesslike way. "Eunice, clear the table. Signor Pinocchio and his cricket will be eating the special diet from now on." The ewe placed the dishes and plates on the sideboard; then she cleared away our first breakfast, which we had not touched.

I reached for the first dish: a baked apple dripping with chocolate sauce. It looked and smelled delicious. I examined the second dish: stewed figs drenched in honey and cream, sprinkled with grated chocolate. Even better! With anticipation I lifted the lid from the third dish: sliced ham smothered with more chocolate sauce. I knew I was going to like this diet, but I was curious about the choice of dishes.

"Doctor Moro, I never would have expected a diet to be so appetizing! I'd like to know how this fare will nourish the human within me and starve the lower nature."

"I don't mind sharing with you the reasons I selected these foods; I believe scientific knowledge should be open to all, that nothing should be kept secret.

"I chose baked apple because it was the food of the first man and woman, Adamo and Eva. They ate the apple uncooked, of course, but I serve only cooked food to those who would become human, for only human beings cook food.

"I settled on figs sweetened with cream and honey for the second course because they were the favorite dessert of the Caesars. In the centuries before Rome became Christian the Roman Senate proclaimed the Caesars gods. I reason that the food of men who became gods might help animals become men.

"As for ham, I deem the pig to be the most intelligent and pure of animals whose flesh is eaten. Ordinary thinkers disagree; they think the pig must be stupid and unclean because it eats garbage and wallows in the mud. But that shows the pig's almost human cunning, by developing a reputation for uncleanness the pig avoids being eaten by Jews and Muslims.

"I have seasoned all three dishes with chocolate. Chocolate is the flavoring most suited to the human soul. Chocolate will be your drink as well. You do like chocolate, don't you?"

"I have a passion for chocolate, Doctor," I admitted.

"There you go," he beamed, "I told you that you have a little bit of human nature inside you already, even though you are made of wood. And your friend, insect though he is, has a bit of the human in him too—just look at him!"

"I have seasoned all three dishes with chocolate. Chocolate is the flavoring most suited to the human soul. Chocolate will be your drink as well. You do like chocolate, don't you?"
"I have a passion for chocolate, Doctor," I admitted.

I turned to Gregorio. He had already buried his face in the chocolate sauce lapping around the ham. When he realized we were watching him, my friend raised his head and looked at us sheepishly, the sweet brown liquid running down his mandibles and dripping back onto the platter.

"Pardon me," he apologized in a thick voice, "I was seized by an overpowering urge to get started on breakfast while you two talked."

"Go ahead with your meal," Doctor Moro said. "I'll come back when it's time to expose you to uplifting music and art."

Without bothering to reply, Gregorio and I fell to our breakfast and devoured it in a matter of minutes, like animals.

Chapter 29

We ate the same food three times a day for two weeks without once tiring of it. I could never get enough chocolate!

The music was another matter. Doctor Moro made us listen to chamber music after every meal. Even the greatest composers became unpalatable after a steady diet of their works. The Doctor started us on Mozart, but when he sensed we were tiring of him he had the musicians switch to Schubert, then to Beethoven, and finally to Brahms. The players looked very distinguished in black dinner jackets and ties. Their long hair swept back with a flourish over the crowns of their heads all the way down to their shoulders. Not until the third day did I realize with a sudden start that they were, or had been, lions. The Doctor had done a good piece of work with them. They looked the part and played well, considering that their fingers were still thick and furry. At times I thought I heard an untrimmed claw catch on a string, but I could never be sure the part was not scored pizzicato.

After listening to the music of the immortals for an hour the Doctor would walk us through his private picture gallery. He had chosen his paintings and watercolors for their noble themes, and as we stopped in front of each one he would invite us to drink deeply with our eyes and fortify our thirsty souls. Following our stroll through the art gallery we would return to our room to rest and meditate on what we had heard and seen.

Well before the fourteenth day, I knew that the Method of Inner Change was not working. I looked the same, but I was different inside, and not for the better. I didn't feel noble at all, but vulgar and crude. I had consumed so much chocolate that the bubbling brown liquid rose from my heart to my tongue. I found myself uttering coarse words and oaths without even thinking what I was saying. Father hadn't raised me to use foul language, and it shamed me when I caught myself doing it. Doctor Moro said chocolate was refined; but refined sin is still sin, and it brought out the worst in me.

The Method of Inner Change also had an unexpected effect on Gregorio. My friend was growing. As soon as we began the special diet he began to swell. Gregorio went through ten molts in thirteen days and recovered his full height by day thirteen; but he remained a cricket, a cricket the size of a ten year-old boy. He also began to drool chocolate sauce when he became excited or agitated, the way grasshoppers drool tobacco juice.

"I'm afraid of the changes in me, Pinocchio," Gregorio confessed when we retired to our room on the evening of the thirteenth day. "I'm more revolting and loathsome and less like a human being than before."

"Don't you think regaining your height is a step in the right direction?" I asked.

"Not if being bigger makes me a bigger sinner," he replied. "Just look at me: I'm simply slobbering sin. And what about the language I've heard coming out of your mouth these past few days? Pinocchio, the Doctor's experiment is more than a failure; it's made things worse. We've got to get out of here tomorrow."

After what I just told you, you'd think I'd have agreed with Gregorio at once. Instead, I felt resentful and obstinate. Fumes from the simmering chocolate had begun to darken my brain, like a ham hanging in a smokehouse.

"I'll admit that some of the things I've heard myself say have distressed me, but I don't think I've really become worse," I retorted. "That's just the chocolate talking; it's not the real me. To be frank, I'm enjoying the Doctor's treatment. I'm not being changed into a real boy but I'm having a wonderful time. I want to stay here."

"You'll have a wonderful time till your money runs out; then what will happen? You'll have a month left at the most before you run down. Do you want to die without seeing your father again? Have you given up hope of becoming a real boy? Pinocchio, I believe you've forgotten our quest. You've become addicted to chocolate and it's put your brain to sleep. Snap out of your sweet brown stupor!"

Gregorio's warning cut through the chocolate fog and awakened me to my danger like the baying of the hound cuts through the morning mist and wakes the sleeping fox. He was right: the very chocolate I loved so much would be the death of me. Doctor Moro was feeding me sin, and I was loving it.

I slapped my wooden cheeks to clear my head. "How could I have been such a fool?" I asked no one in particular. "Everywhere we've gone I've fallen into some sort of sin; now I've surpassed all my earlier idiocy by positively devouring the stuff. Staying here would be sure, sweet death for us. You're right as usual, Gregorio. We must leave this island quick as we can."

The next morning we told Doctor Moro that his treatment had been a failure and that we intended to return to Portofino that very day, the two-week trial being ended. He listened to us, a faint smile on his face.

"I'm afraid that will be impossible," he replied with a cruel chuckle. "The sea is too rough for sailing today. I think it will be too rough for several weeks. You'll have to stay here for at least three more weeks, at a ducat a day, each."

I looked out to sea. The water was calm as glass.

"Doctor, you can't be serious. Even I could sail a boat on that pond."

"Listen to me, you fool," he answered in a voice cold as ice and hard as flint. "I have no intention of letting you leave my island. You and the cricket are providing me with valuable experimental evidence and fine gold ducats as well. Your only choice is whether you will continue or refuse to proceed with the Method of Inner Change. If you choose to continue the experiment, all will be as it has been for the past two weeks: you will eat delicious food and enjoy fine music and art. I'll even continue the treatment at no charge after you run out of money. If you refuse to proceed, my servants will bind you hand and foot—that would be foreleg and foot for you, cricket—and throw you from the top of the cliff into the sea. I hope you have enough sense to cooperate, for I'm most anxious to see how the experiment turns out. You know, you are the first subjects to undergo the Method of Internal Change."

"We bow to your superior force, Doctor," Gregorio said before I could reply. "We ask only that you waive further charges and allow us to keep the little money we still have. If the Method of Inner Change succeeds you will earn a fortune beyond anything you've known, and Pinocchio's few coins will mean nothing to you. If the experiment fails, Pinocchio will die and you will have the ducats anyway."

"Well, well; you're reasoning like a human being already," beamed the Doctor. "Agreed. Back to your room now, and let's hear no more about leaving the island. Breakfast will be served in a half-hour as usual."

Chapter 29

Gregorio had to have some scheme. I asked him about it in the privacy of our room.

"We must not eat any of those fatal delicacies today—we'll find some way to dispose of them. Tonight we'll take the sloop and flee this lunatic's island." I had to praise Gregorio for quick thinking. The chocolate had altered his body, but it had not affected his brain as it had mine. Before the breakfast bell rang we had devised an ingenious plan to escape.

It turned out to be much easier to avoid eating Doctor Moro's special food than I imagined. The Doctor never ate with us; the only occupants of the special dining room were Gregorio, the maid, and I. After the maid set the tray on the table I stopped her as she turned to go.

"My dear woman, my cricket and I are not feeling well today; we're not at all hungry. Would you like to sample this rich fare?" The ewe poked her finger in the baked apple and licked it. Her eyes brightened and she bleated softly with pleasure.

"Go ahead, eat it all," I encouraged her. "We won't tell the Doctor. You may have our lunch, too, if we're not feeling better." The maid needed no further persuading. She gulped all three dishes down, even the ham. When she had finished, she wiped her mouth with her wooly arm and began to clear away the dishes as though nothing unusual had happened.

At lunch we were surprised to see the ewe appear with two other sheep, who also wore the traditional black and white maid's outfit. I told them we still felt ill and invited all three to share our meal. The newcomers were reluctant.

"It's perfectly all right," I assured them. "Eunice has already eaten our breakfast." When they heard that, and saw that their friend had already begun to eat, her friends willingly joined her in polishing off our lunch. Sheep are such followers! While the newcomers were clearing the table I asked Eunice to bring us some chicken broth and leafy green vegetables for supper instead of the special diet. I promised that she and her friends could consume our regular dinner somewhere in secret. The maid found this proposal agreeable and did as she was told. We were able to pass the whole day without eating any chocolate.

We both felt better that evening, actually clear-headed and energetic. I hadn't realized how much chocolate sapped my strength and befogged my brain. Now I felt fit and ready to make a break from the island as soon as all its inhabitants were asleep.

The waxing moon was already high in the sky when the last lights in the villa went out. Gregorio and I stole silently from our room and tiptoed down the hall to the main entrance. We slipped out onto the veranda and closed the door noiselessly behind us. Gregorio and I waited in the shadows another half-hour to be sure everyone was asleep, then made for the belt of pine trees encircling the compound. Once past the pines, we crawled through the grass down to the dock where the sloop was tied up. By that time a small cloud lay over the moon and we could move around openly.

I was always a curious boy, even when I was a puppet. I had watched Doctor Moro's crew handle the tiller and sails on our passage to the island and was confident Gregorio and I could sail the sloop back to the mainland over such a calm, starlit sea. I untied the mooring line and sculled the sloop away from the dock. Then I raised the sails and sat down in the stern with one hand on the tiller and the other on the mainsail sheet.

The sails filled with wind and the sloop glided away from the dark island. I was surprised at how stiff the breeze was away from the shelter of the cliffs and remarked on this to Gregorio, who was handling the headsail from the front of the cockpit.

"It's more than getting out from the lee of the island, Pinocchio," said my friend. "The wind is picking up. Just look at the sky now."

I looked up and saw large clouds scudding swiftly northward. As I gazed at the heavens a huge black pall spread over the sky from one horizon to the other, extinguishing the moon and stars. Rain began to fall, first large drops splashing one by one on the deck, then a drenching, wind-driven downpour. The wind set the surface of the sea heaving and tossing. I began to get sick.

"Gregorio! I'm too ill to steer!" I called weakly. I looked forward and saw my friend leaning over the side, moaning, chocolate dribbling from his mouth into the sea. His forelegs held his head; the headsail flapped uncontrollably in the gale. I felt dizzy and dropped the mainsail sheet. I wrapped my arms around the tiller to keep from tumbling overboard—I had no thought to steer! The sloop and our fate were out of our control. We were at the mercy of the storm and of the Lord.

"It's more than getting out from the lee of the island, Pinocchio," said my friend. "The wind is picking up. Just look at the sky now."

Chapter 30

The storm raged till near morning, but I remember little of it. All night long I was conscious only of my throbbing head and tossing stomach. In the end it was the blessed morning sun that penetrated my soul and drew me out of my misery. I sat up and blinked. The sea was calm, the sky was blue, the air was warm and still. I raised my eyes to the top of the mast. Only a few tatters of canvas hung there. The sails were gone, ripped off by the fierce winds. I heard a moan and looked down. Gregorio lay on his back in the bottom of the boat, wiggling his legs as he tried to turn over. My friend was weak but alive. We had survived the storm.

"Gregorio!" I whispered feebly. "The tempest is over. God preserved us."

A bloated and soggy cricket lifted his head and tried to smile. "Yes," he agreed, "He did not let us perish. For most of the night, though, I wished for nothing so much as a quick death. Where are we?"

I looked ahead—and practically jumped out of the boat. Less than a mile ahead of us an island rose above the calm waters. My heart sank. The gentle current was bearing us back to Doctor Moro.

"Gregorio! The sea is returning us to our watery prison!" I grasped my friend's carapace and helped him roll over. He peered ahead with his hundred eyes, then smiled.

"No, Pinocchio, it's not Doctor Moro's island. The cliffs look the same, but it's a different island."

He was right. The rocky mass looming up before us looked very much like Doctor Moro's island, but a small village, not a lone villa, huddled against the shore. The island ahead was not the ocean laboratory we had fled; but what was it? Doctor Moro had assured us that there were no other islands in the gulf.

Our helpless vessel drifted straight towards the village dock. A sloop in dire need of paint bobbed up and down at dockside, and three seamen sat on the dock soaking in the sun, smoking their pipes and whittling nothing in particular. When we were a few yards away one of the men stood up and motioned for me to throw him the mooring line. He made the line fast, and Gregorio and I painfully hauled ourselves up the rope ladder the man threw down to us.

"Were you out in the storm all night?" he asked, astonished.

"Yes," I answered, "We got caught by surprise a little before midnight."

"I take my hat off to you and to your seamanship, Signor," the sailor replied. "My sloop would have gone under, and it's bigger than yours."

"Thank you," I responded with a self-satisfied smile. I should have thanked the gracious Lord for our deliverance instead of accepting the man's praise myself, but no sooner were my feet on the solid dock than the chocolate within once again began to fume and fill my head.

"Where are we?" I asked the sailors. "I thought the only island in these waters was the island of Doctor Moro. We came from there, and his island looks like the mirror image of this one."

"Oh, you came from Doctor Moro's island, did you?" laughed another seaman, a grizzled old salt. "Well, it's really very near here, though you can't see it unless you climb to the top of the cliffs. You might be surprised what you would see if you did that." The speaker's companions burst out laughing at his reply. We were to find out why all too soon.

"No, thank you," I replied, "we've had quite enough of Doctor Moro. We want to get back to Genoa as soon as possible. As you can see, our sail is gone. Is there a sailmaker on the island?"

"No; our little village is much too small," answered the third sailor, without bothering to get up. "If you want to leave here you'll have to wait for the Portofino ferry. It calls on Mondays and Fridays. Today is Saturday, so you'll have a two-day wait."

"I wouldn't have thought this island big enough to merit two ferry trips a week."

"Oh, we have a youth hostel on the island," explained the second seaman. "Boys come here on school holiday. We also breed donkeys here. Those are our two means of livelihood, and what with boys coming and donkeys going we have a lot of ferry traffic."

"What an odd combination of industries!" I exclaimed. My thoughts returned to Genoa. "Is there no other way to get back to Portofino? Perhaps I could hire you to take me in your boat."

"No, that would be impossible; you see, it's not our boat. Everything on the island including this boat belongs to Signor Orom. Signor Orom runs the hostel and owns the breeding farm."

"Then I'll deal with him."

"He's not here now. Signor Orom lives on the other side of the island. We never know when he's going to pay us a visit. You'll have to deal with his steward, the Coachman."

"Where can we find this Coachman?"

"He's not on the island now, either. He arrives Monday with a new group of boys."

"But this isn't the holiday season," I said.

"That's as may be," the man replied, "but they come all year long just the same. I notice *you're* not in school. Boys who come here don't like school any more than you do."

The three men tossed the sticks they were whittling into the water and folded up their jackknives.

"Signor, we'd talk longer but we've a lot to do before the Coachman returns," said the first seaman. "If he finds we've been idle, we'll be sorry for it. You'll have to stay at the hostel till Monday. There are no other inns or rooms on our little island."

Since there was nothing else to do, we said goodbye to the seamen and turned to walk ashore. Then my eyes fell on a familiar sight that sent my heart plunging to my stomach. A fourth seaman, who had been sitting out of sight behind a barrel, rose to say good day with the others. He was wearing my father's old hat!

Gregorio saw the hat at the same instant I did and squealed, "Pinocchio! That man is wearing your father's hat!"

"Where did you get that hat?" I shrieked.

"Strange you should ask, Signor. I found it on the beach three weeks ago. I washed the salt out and now it's as good as new."

"That's my father's hat!" I cried. "He must have gone down at sea!"

The seamen murmured their sympathy but I scarcely heard them. My dear father, the man who gave me life and loved me, was dead! I collapsed on the dock in sobs. Who would have thought such a flow of tears could gush from such well-seasoned wood?

Gregorio put a foreleg around my shaking shoulders and sat silently beside me. After a while, he began to speak softly and gently.

"Pinocchio, it's still possible your father is alive. In my opinion, it's even likely. This man found his hat, not his body. Doctor Moro is an evil man, but he had reason on his side when he said that either the raft or the body was bound to surface if your father had drowned. It's easy enough to lose a hat in the stiff sea breeze."

I ran back to the seamen and questioned them about Father. They assured me that neither raft nor body had washed up on the beaches of their little island. The seaman, feeling sorry for me, gave me Father's hat.

Gregorio and I walked up the hill. I said nothing but I was thinking plenty. My friend meant well with his words of assurance, but in my heart I felt I would never see Father again. He was dead, I was sure of it. His God had let him down; He had let me down too. But what did it matter? I had only a month left before my spring unwound completely. Gabriela was but a beautiful, painful memory. Doctor Moro had proved to be a quack; Giovanni had not appeared to save me. I gave up hope.

We rounded a bend in the path and the hostel came into view, a two-story lodge at the end of the road. Behind the lodge stretched a line of low stables fronting on a long fenced area. At least three dozen donkeys were milling around in this corral, braying mournfully. We saw no one as we approached the lodge.

I stopped on the porch before we entered the hostel.

"Gregorio, I'm too weary and discouraged to return to Genoa Monday. If Father is really on a ship on its way back to Genoa, which I doubt, he won't get there for a week. I want to rest here for a few days and heal my mind. Maybe I can recover enough strength to continue our quest."

With the instinct of a large intelligent insect, my friend knew that it was useless to argue with me in that state of mind.

"Very well; we'll stay here a little while, but no more than a week. The angel Gabriele said you could go wherever you wanted; Giovanni will find you. I guess he can find you here as well as in Genoa. It doesn't matter to me. Wherever I am, I'm too loathsome for God to look on me with grace. Only don't let yourself fall deeper into sin while you're resting, or you may fall so low that He won't care to save you either."

I pushed the door open and we entered the lodge. Seeing no one, I crossed the lobby to the main desk and banged loudly on the bell. A muffled noise from the back of the building told us we had been heard. Soon a round man about fifty years old stepped through

We rounded a bend in the path and the hostel came into view, a two-story lodge at the end of the road. Behind the lodge stretched a line of low stables fronting on a long fenced area.

a door in front of me. When he saw me, he bustled around the end of the desk and hurried forward to greet me. Then he saw Gregorio and stopped at once, some six feet from us.

"'Pon my soul, what have we here? Are you entertainers looking for work? How did you get here, anyway? The ferry don't come till Monday, and I know you didn't get off Friday's boat. Signor, is that, uh, your pet? It don't bite, does it? No, it can't be a real cricket! You must be a ventriloquist! I suppose you make the cricket talk. To tell the truth, you look more like you ought to be the dummy—nothin' personal in that remark, you understand. I'd like to see your act, but I don't have permission to hire nobody. You'll have to wait till the Coachman comes back. He'll be here Monday. You can stay in the lodge unless your cricket really is a bug. We don't take no pets, Signor, and we don't book no animal acts."

"My name is Pinocchio, my good man, and this is my friend, Gregorio. He is as much a real boy as I am."

As soon as the words left my mouth my nose started to tingle. I covered it with my hand so the clerk wouldn't see it growing; I could feel it begin to swell already. (When I finally dared to look in a mirror, I saw that it was a good quarter-inch longer.) I hadn't told an outright lie, but my remarks were misleading—as I had meant them to be. It was clear that the Lord didn't think much of my cleverness, for He visited my sin upon my face immediately.

I succeeded in deceiving the clerk. He was relieved by my words of assurance and gladly accepted seven lire for a week's food and lodging for Gregorio and me. When I remarked on how reasonable the rates were, the clerk replied that Signor Orom made little money from the boys' resort.

"The hostel is his hobby. The Boss makes his profit from selling donkeys to the mainland."

"I'm surprised the stables are so close to the lodge," I remarked. "Don't the braying and the smell and the dust annoy the guests?"

"They don't seem to," the clerk replied. "Noise and stink and dirt never bothered no real boy I ever knew. Besides, the hostel business and the donkey business is related, so to speak."

As soon as he said that, a shadow of alarm crossed the clerk's face. He quickly added, "What I mean is, the boys ride the donkeys all over the island. It's a big part of their fun."

I sensed dimly that there was more to the connection between the resort and the donkeys than he was willing to reveal. But then the man did something that made me forget all about boys and donkeys: he offered me a chocolate candy.

"Here, have one of these while you sign the guest book. It's a welcoming touch for our guests."

After all we had gone through on Doctor Moro's island, the mere mention of chocolate should have turned my stomach, but desire for the sweet poison sprang to life in me again. If it hadn't been for Gregorio, I would have wolfed the bonbon down in a single gulp.

"Pinocchio! We've sworn off chocolate forever, remember?"

"Yes, that's right. Thank you anyway, innkeeper."

I signed the book and we went to find our room. A week of rest, then we would plod on hopelessly in search of Father till I ran down. Remember, by then I had given up all hope of becoming a real boy.

Chapter 31

Gregorio and I were exhausted after our fight with the sea and slept most of Saturday and Sunday. We slept in Monday, too, until the shouts and whoops of boys running up and down the halls aroused us.

"It sounds like the ferry has come in," Gregorio said, yawning with wide-open mandibles and stretching two pairs of legs.

"I think you're right," I agreed, rubbing my eyes and swinging my legs over the side of the bed. "Let's go find the Coachman."

We descended to the lobby, where we found a round, red-faced man surrounded by a surging crowd of boys. They were loud and disorderly, and the man was laughing and shouting right along with them. His long coat, top hat, boots, and gloves left no doubt that this jolly fellow was indeed the Coachman.

"Help yourselves to anything you want in the kitchen, lads," he told the boys. "Don't worry about washing up first and don't worry about keeping things clean. While you're here you can live just as you want."

When he saw us the Coachman left the boys to run amuck and walked over to the foot of the staircase to greet us.

"Ah, you must be our unexpected guests! My desk clerk told me we had two visitors from the ocean. Who might you be, and how did you come here?"

I told him of our quest to become real boys and of our search for Father, and related our adventures from Portofino until our arrival on the island.

"We're too tired to continue on our way just yet; and frankly, I'm too downhearted."

"Glad to have you!" he exclaimed. "You'll find our little retreat just the place to rest and raise your spirits again. You just join the other boys in their fun. We call our resort Pleasure Island because our guests can do what they please here. Follow the urgings of your nature. There's no one here to say no or scold or give you a licking. Sleep in as late as you want and stay up as late as you want; dump your vegetables on the floor and eat sweets all day long; be rude and crude and shout whenever grownups would tell you to whisper; ride donkeys wherever you want; do all the exciting things your mother calls dangerous. This is a place for boys to live without rules. Here, have some chocolate candy." The Coachman held out a bag of bonbons.

"No, thank you. My friend, Gregorio, and I have sworn off chocolate. It seems to bring out the worst in us."

"Then try these candies instead." he replied, producing a shiny pink box. I removed the lid and saw that the box contained plump, white candies.

"What are they?" I asked.

"They're white chocolate creams. White chocolate is highly refined and much more expensive than brown chocolate. With white chocolate you get all the delicious chocolate flavor but none of the degrading coarseness of the native brown variety. It is very sophisticated; I'm sure it will please sensitive souls like yourselves."

Gregorio and I looked at one another: Was white chocolate really harmless? Could we have all the pleasures of the chocolate we so enjoyed without suffering its ill effects? There was no way to know but to try it.

"Thank you. We'll both try one, but only one," I replied. I popped a bonbon in my mouth and crushed its soft chocolate shell with my teeth; I rolled the syrup around on my tongue and smacked my lips. It was so good! I hoped with my whole heart that all the sin had been refined out of white chocolate, for I dearly wanted to gorge on it during our week on the island. I looked at Gregorio. His hundred eyes gleamed with satisfaction as he wiped a mandible with a foreleg.

"There will always be a box of these candies under the reception desk if you get hungry between meals," the Coachman said. "I repeat: Do what you want here. You'll pay me for it at the end."

"Oh, we paid in advance," I told him.

"That wasn't necessary, Signori," the Coachmen laughed, "We're used to collecting what is due us at the end of a stay. Enjoy yourselves while you can." Still chuckling, the Coachman turned away and began to talk to some other boys. I stuffed my pocket with white chocolate creams and motioned to Gregorio to follow me out the door.

We strolled around in the warm sunshine, bound for nowhere in particular. When we were well away from the hostel, Gregorio asked me, "What did the Coachman mean, 'Enjoy yourselves while you can'?"

"I suppose he meant while we're on the island," I answered. "What else could he mean?"

"I don't know," my friend replied. "It just seemed like an odd thing to say." Before long we would find out exactly what the Coachman's words meant.

The boys' arrival made our stay more interesting for a day or so. They swaggered around the lodge bragging how strong, clever, and bad they were. The biggest toughs tried to prove it by swearing, gambling, and fighting from the moment they arrived. When they weren't causing trouble they were stuffing themselves with pastries and candy, above all, chocolate. A few bullies who had made themselves masters of the other boys thought to show me who was boss, but I knew enough from fighting with the Mountaineers to give them all a nasty surprise. My challengers retreated with swollen lips and bloody noses, to wonder why hitting me bruised their knuckles so. One boy who tried to rough up Gregorio got a powerful kick in the jaw that actually knocked out two teeth. After that they left us alone.

Except for Monday, when the ferry arrived, our week on the island was so quiet it was boring. We ate a lot of white chocolate creams and took long donkey rides to pass the time. I never saw such sad donkeys! They were fat and sleek, and appeared to be well cared for; yet tears welled up in their huge black eyes, and their braying was heart-rending, like the lament of one who has suffered a loss never to be recovered.

After lunch Wednesday, when everyone else was taking the daily siesta, Gregorio and I were tossing on our beds, too bored to sleep. I suggested another donkey ride to kill time and my friend agreed. We slipped quietly out of the lodge so as not to wake the other boys and made for the stables. There we saddled a pair of donkeys and started up the trail to the cliffs, keeping our mounts quiet with a couple of bonbons. After plodding for a time along a path that wound through a jumble of boulders at the base of the cliffs, I brought up an idea I had been turning over in my mind for a day or two.

"Let's try to make our way to the top of the ridge. I'd like to see if we can spot Doctor Moro's island." My friend replied that he had been thinking the same thing. We clip-clopped to one end of the island and then back again to the other side, keeping our eyes open for an upward-tending trail, but we found none.

"We'd better be getting back, Pinocchio," said Gregorio after a couple of hours. "Look at that squall coming off the water."

I scarcely had time to lift my eyes toward the sea when the curtain of rain hit us. We dug our heels into the sides of our mounts and made for some brush growing up against the rocky wall. When we reached our refuge we found it to be even better than it looked from the trail, for the thicket covered the mouth of a cave that no one could see from below. We tried to lead the donkeys into the rock shelter. When they saw the cave, they planted their feet and wouldn't go another step forward. I looked into their eyes, expecting to see stubborn obstinacy. I was surprised to find them looking back at me with fear in their eyes.

"Pinocchio, the donkeys know this cave," said Gregorio. "They seem afraid of it."

"So it seems," I replied, "but I can't see why—just brute stupidity, I imagine. Let them shiver in the rain if they want to. We've got no reason to stand out in the open with them. Come on."

Dismounting, we left the beasts outside to fend for themselves and hurried into the cave. It was about twenty feet deep and not at all dark. This particular cave was like many others along the base of the cliffs that we had explored in the past several days except for one striking and curious feature: in the back of the cave was an iron door. I tugged on its handle and it yielded to my pull. Gregorio and I forgot all about the donkeys and the rain and the Coachman. Like real boys, we had to know what was behind the door. I pulled it full open and we stepped through it.

Before us a ramp sloped downward, running straight into the stony heart of the island. Leaving the door open for light, we started down the ramp. The light quickly dimmed to darkness as we went further in. The ramp was broad, well paved, and led us on—to where? We kept going—what was there to be afraid of?

We had walked for no more than ten minutes when the floor beneath our feet leveled out. By my reckoning we had passed under the island's rocky spine and were more or less at sea level on the other side. A few more paces and my nose ran into a hard surface. We had reached the end of the tunnel. I ran my hands over the

"Pinocchio, the donkeys know this cave," said Gregorio. "They seem afraid of it."

unseen wall in front of me and my fingers soon closed over the handle of another door. It turned freely.

"Well, Gregorio, I've found the door at this end. Are you ready to see what's on the other side?"

"Of course. What do you suppose we'll find?"

"Lots of green grass, I imagine. It's obvious the donkeys know this place. There's no way over the ridge to the other side; we must be on the path the herdsmen use to bring the beasts from one side of the island to the other. It's clear they're terrified by the darkness. Let's see if I'm right."

I opened the door and found myself looking into Doctor Moro's wine cellar.

Chapter 32

We looked at each other, confused and speechless. We could not believe what lay before us. We had entered Doctor Moro's wine cellar from the rear—through the one door I found locked when we searched his villa. No wonder the seamen on the dock laughed when I told them we had escaped from Doctor Moro: Signor Orom's island was but the backside of Doctor Moro's island!

Gregorio was the first to grasp the full meaning of our discovery. "Pinocchio," he whispered, "Orom is Moro spelled backwards. Signor Orom and Doctor Moro are one and the same. Can his business on this side of the island be less sinister than his work on the other side? The boys' hostel and donkey ranch have to be connected with the surgical laboratory in some insane and horrible scheme."

I held my finger to my lips and motioned for my friend to follow me. I quietly shut the door; then we ran swiftly and softly up the dark tunnel. We didn't slow down till we neared the mouth of the cave.

The squall had passed over the island and the sky was bright and blue again. Our terrified donkeys stood right where we had left them, their wet hides steaming in the sun. We climbed up on the beasts and headed down the trail towards the lodge. Only when we were well away from the cave did I dare to answer my friend.

"You're right, Gregorio; Doctor Moro's mad project must extend to this side of the island, too. But we've explored the lodge, the village, and every other corner of this island and we haven't found anything like a surgery or operating room. Whatever the Doctor is doing here, it isn't what he's doing on the other side."

We were about a quarter-mile from the stables when we heard the donkeys bawling. Pandemonium reigned in the corral. The braying and hee-hawing was three times louder than ever before, but it wasn't the din alone that stopped our donkeys in their tracks. Every bray overflowed with panic and fear, every hee-haw was filled with shock and horror. Dread nearly froze our own hearts as we heard the horrible moaning and wailing. We didn't even think of trying to spur our terror-stricken mounts forward; we knew as well as they did that something was very, very wrong.

Dismounting, we approached the pens with stealth, flitting from bush to bush. We reached the back of the stables unseen. When we peeked around the corner at the corral, all the pieces of the puzzle fell together. Three dozen panic-stricken boys were running every which way, three dozen boys who had grown donkey ears and tails, three dozen boys becoming donkeys before our goggling eyes. Those who had only begun to change were crying and moaning and calling for help with human voices; those whose heads were fully transformed were braying piteously. The Coachman stood in the middle of the corral, laughing as always, cracking a braided leather whip with a horseshoe nail in the end. The innkeeper and a half-dozen other servants stood near him, whips in hand.

"What's the matter, boys? You were donkeys before you ever came here. We've just let Signor Orom's Method of Inner Change have its way with you. We gave your donkey natures their way and fed your donkey natures the food they loved; now your donkey natures have taken over. Your outer form finally matches your inner selves. Did you really think you could do just as your lower nature pleased and look the same to the world?"

The donkeys answered their tormentor with a chorus of hee-haws. They didn't bray with gusto like fat donkeys that have eaten their fill, nor with defiance like sullen beasts of burden that refuse to go another step; they bawled in craven fear like prisoners of war begging for their lives.

"You plead for mercy? Well, Signor Orom will have mercy on one or two of you. He'll take you to a clinic where the good Doctor Moro will turn you back into human beings by means of scalpel and suture—what he calls it the Method of Outer Change. Doctor Moro and Signor Orom are one and the same person, boys. He can wound, but he can also heal. Each of you should pray that he will be one of the favored few. The rest of you can look forward to being sold to some kind master on the mainland. Doctor Moro would like to restore you all, but he needs money to finance his research. Science is costly, boys; so even those sold will have a part in the advancement of knowledge. Let that thought console you while you eat your hay tonight!"

Chapter 32

One of the Coachman's servants tugged on his sleeve, and the wicked man stopped mocking the boys, who had all turned completely into donkeys by now.

"Boss, two of the animals is missing; I just counted. Also, I ain't seen that wooden kid and his big bug since lunch."

"Aldo saw them heading for the stables at the siesta hour; they must be out riding. Search the island till you find them; then bind them and bring them down to the dock. There you are to weigh them down with rocks and cast them into the sea. Those are special orders from the Doctor."

Gregorio and I turned and ran uphill through the scrub, not stopping till we were out of earshot of the stables. Panting for breath, I mused out loud, "Where can we go? We could double back to the dock and try to steal a boat, but the dock is the place they will watch most carefully."

Gregorio interrupted my panicky meditation. "I think our only chance, small though it may be, is to return to Doctor Moro's side of the island. That's the last place they'd think of looking for us. There was another boat tied up to the dock, remember? Maybe it's still there. We could steal it and attempt a second escape by sea."

Insect though he was, Gregorio had the brains of our partnership. His scheme was desperate, and promised little hope of success, but it was the only plan that offered any hope at all. We ran towards the tunnel. I had a hard time of it, stumbling over rocks and roots, gasping almost as loudly as a donkey brays. Gregorio had the advantage of me, hopping easily by my side.

I had to slow down, so Gregorio went on ahead to find the cave. Too soon he came hopping back, all eyes wide with fright. "It's too late! Doctor Moro himself and a band of those made-over beasts have left the cave and are almost upon us!"

We dove off the path and sought somewhere to hide in the brush. Just in time! We lay flat against the ground no more than five yards from the path and watched Doctor Moro and a dozen of his servants tramp past us on their way to the donkey pens.

"We haven't much time," I whispered after they disappeared down the path. "He'll know we're at large in ten minutes at most. We've got to see if they left the tunnel unguarded." Keeping off the trail, we pressed on uphill through the scrub. When we arrived at the cave we saw that the Doctor had left two of his dog-seamen there as watchers.

"Come on," I said, turning to the right. "We're going to climb this cliff. If we can't go under the ridge we'll go over it. The sailors talked as though they'd been to the top. There must be a way."

We wound our way along the foot of the cliff for nearly a mile before we found a way up. We discovered it almost by accident. Gregorio happened to look up and almost shouted in surprise: "Above you, Pinocchio! Stairs!"

I looked up where Gregorio was pointing and whistled in surprise. A stone staircase zig-zagged down the side of the rock face from above. The steps ended abruptly at a landing fifteen feet above my head. The bottom course of steps had collapsed, adding a few stones to the talus spreading out from the foot of the cliff.

"I can hop to the bottom landing," my friend said excitedly. "Take off your clothes and tie them together to make a rope. I'll tie the rope to that shale outcropping by the landing; it looks solid from here. Then you can climb up to me."

Didn't I tell you Gregorio had brains enough for both of us? I did as he said and soon we both stood on the landing. I put my clothes on as quickly as possible—I was a sinner, and only a wooden boy at that, but I knew how to blush—and we began our climb up the stairs.

No doubt you, who were born real boys and girls, have already forseen the great risk we took on the stairs. The higher we climbed, the more visible we were to anyone who might glance up at the great stone curtain looming above the island. We felt like flies crawling across a hanging slab of meat in full view of the butcher. All we could do was keep toiling upwards, back and forth across the face of the cliff, hoping to reach the crest before we were seen.

It seemed like we were exposed to all below for an hour, but in fact we reached the top of the steps in no more than ten minutes. We were delighted to find the ridge flat on top and covered with plenty of boulders where we could rest for a few minutes out of sight of hostile eyes. We sat with our backs to a large limestone mass and waited for our hearts to slow down.

I felt wearier than I had ever felt before. My spring had only three weeks of life left in it and the climb had used up a good half-day of that. We closed our eyes and soaked in the afternoon sun. We listened for the sounds of our pursuers but heard only the faint cry of seabirds. "I don't hear anything below, Gregorio. Maybe no one spotted us."

Before Gregorio could reply a cold shadow fell over us. Our eyes popped open and beheld Doctor Moro standing above us, his mouth twisted upward in a cruel grin. Behind him hulked the dog-sailors. We jumped to our feet, weariness forgotten, and started to back away. The Doctor and his crew advanced on us with slow, steady pace. We retreated step by step until we found ourselves backed onto a narrow tongue of rock at the very end of the ridge. The cliffs dropped away on three sides. We were trapped!

Before Gregorio could reply a cold shadow fell over us. Our eyes popped open and beheld Doctor Moro standing above us, his mouth twisted upward in a cruel grin. Behind him hulked the dog-sailors.

Chapter 33

Doctor Moro and his crew stopped ten feet from the end of the promontory. "How did you find us?" I asked. "And how did you come upon us without our hearing you?"

"I don't mind answering your questions, young fool; it's very much like giving a condemned prisoner whatever he wants for his last meal. We tracked you to the stairs by following the trail of chocolate your friend dribbled. Even white chocolate makes dirty brown tobacco juice, cricket. We had no need to follow you up the broken stairs, for I have a private passageway climbing up through the heart of the island to a lookout on the summit behind me. I knew you found my tunnel—those chocolate drippings again—but you didn't find my secret stairs, so I was able to surprise you.

"It's too bad you weren't willing to cooperate in my experiments, but it's too late to think about what might have been. You believe in God? Now would be a good time to pray to this phantom god of yours. In just one minute, my loyal servants are going to throw you into the sea."

So this was to be my end. In sixty seconds I would be nothing but shattered driftwood on the beach far below, soon to be scattered by tide and current all across the Gulf of Genoa. I would never see Father again; I would never become a real boy. The Lord had abandoned me to suffer the results of my many sins.

Gregorio replied to the mad Doctor's mockery. "I can't pray as an animal, Doctor, although I once could as a human. But I can show faithfulness and love to my master and friend. Please allow me to give a farewell abraccio to Pinocchio before you kill us."

"Make it quick; you now have only half a minute."

Gregorio gave me a hug with two forelegs and a kiss on both cheeks, a typical Italian abraccio. As he did so he whispered, "Hang on tight, Pinocchio; we have one last chance." I wrapped my arms around Gregorio's waist and hung on for dear life. Then my friend spread his wings and launched himself into the air with a mighty kick of his hindlegs.

Doctor Moro lunged at us, arms raised to catch Gregorio by the ankle. The giant cricket's foot caught the madman on the chin, spinning him around and knocking him sideways. He waved his arms in panic, trying to regain his balance, but could not and plunged over the edge of the precipice. He screamed for an eternity—then silence.

With powerful, steady strokes Gregorio mounted high above the island, circling its ragged summit until the sun was at his back; then he headed east towards the mainland. I held on with fear and hope—how glad I was that my friend was full size again!

The flight to Portofino would be an hour at least. Feeling a bit more secure, I found my voice and began to make conversation.

"How true is the Scripture Barbe Filippo used to recite, 'The wicked has dug a ditch, and fallen into his own pit.' Doctor Moro met with the very end he planned for us."

"True enough," he grunted, "but we may suffer the same fate if this headwind picks up. I'm beginning to tire already. You didn't grow any taller on the chocolate diet, but your pine must have turned to ironwood. I'm sure you've gained twenty pounds."

I was about to come back with a clever retort when Gregorio yelled, "Hang on, Pinocchio! We're under attack!"

I dug my fingers into Gregorio's horny skin; a split-second later a mass of feathers and claws crashed into us. I looked down and saw a stunned seagull spiraling towards the rippling water below. Looking up, I saw a half-dozen birds wheeling in formation overhead; a moment later they began their charge, diving out of the sun with outstretched talons. Gregorio instantly folded his wings and went into free-fall. The screaming gulls overshot us and scattered confused in six directions. Gregorio pulled out of his dive and continued on towards the coast.

"They'll re-group and be back in a minute," my friend panted. "I can't fight and fly at the same time; you'll have to fight for us. I'm going to hold you with my forelegs so you won't fall; you'll be able to use your hands to tie yourself to my back. Then you can do battle with these wicked fowl."

"I'm afraid to let go," I protested in panic, "I'll fall."

"If the gulls pick me apart you'll have nothing to hang on to," he gasped. "You've got to try."

There was no time to argue. With dread, I let go of Gregorio's waist. In spite of growing fatigue, my insect friend gripped me with pinchers of steel. I undid my belt, passed it around Gregorio's body, and hauled myself atop his back. I hooked my feet through the belt and seated myself astride the flying cricket like a knight on a horse. At last I had both hands free.

I shook both fists at the returning gulls, but they continued straight on in V-formation. The lead bird was the biggest. I caught him squarely on the side of the head with my right hand and his limp body plummeted towards the water like a stone. The rest of the flock scattered, but regrouped for another pass at us. The stupid birds stayed in close formation as they approached—if they had attacked from different directions they could have disabled Gregorio and sent us tumbling to the sea. As it was, I landed a solid punch to the keel of one bird, knocking him into his wingman with such force that the first was killed outright and the second was lucky to make a crash landing in the sea. The remaining gulls flew off shrieking; they did not attack again.

"Good work, Pinocchio," chirruped my friend. "You're still the fighter you were when we showed the Mountaineers who ruled the roost." Gregorio tried to sound cheerful, but I detected the strain in his voice. My friend was suffering more than fatigue.

"You're hurt, aren't you?" I asked him. "Tell me the truth."

"One of those lice-ridden scavengers nicked me, but I'll be fine," he replied bravely. "Just let those birds try to attack us again now that we're ready for them."

We flew on in silence for another ten minutes. I sensed we were flying lower and ventured to look down. I could see the choppy waves clearly just fifty feet below.

"Gregorio!" I shouted. "Are you strong enough to make it to the coast?" My friend didn't speak; his labored breathing and the slowing of his wings were answer enough. We were going to crash.

"Gregorio!" I shouted again. "Save your strength and glide down to the water. You carried me through the sky; now I must carry you through the sea. You can float on me."

Gregorio stopped beating his wings and held them out straight. We began to glide gently down to the dark blue water. When we were ten feet above the waves, I jumped into the sea. My crippled friend banked his wings, descended in a slow half-spiral, and landed on my back with a soft thud. I looped the belt loosely around my body. Gregorio was able to grasp to this lifeline with his second pair of legs while resting his head and forelegs on my floating body. All things considered, it was a satisfactory arrangement.

We bobbed gently up and down in silence for a half-hour. Gregorio was too tired to talk and I was pondering our fate. Finally, I spoke my despair.

"Do you realize we haven't prayed to God for days? I gave up on Him entirely when I heard Father was lost at sea, and you've never believed the Lord could bring Himself to care for you. Even so, He delivered us from danger and death time and time again, we who refused to ask Him for help or thank Him after He saved us in spite of our unbelief. Now He's finally run out of patience with us. Let's face it: we're going to perish here in the middle of the sea.

"Swimming to the mainland is out of the question. I suppose the coast is off to our right somewhere, but it's so far away we can't even see it. The current is bearing us out into the gulf. Unless a ship plucks us from the water very soon, you will waterlog and drown and my spring will rust—if it doesn't run down first. God could send Gabriela or Gabriele to save us once again, but I think He's washed His hands of us. We never did see any sign of Giovanni. I guess he never did have a plan to turn us into real boys."

"I think you should pray anyway, Pinocchio," whispered my friend, who was getting soggier and wearier each passing minute. "I still believe God intends to turn you into a real boy, if only for the sake of your godly father. As for me, I'll become fish food like many a cricket before me." Gregorio smiled weakly at his own joke.

I prayed, more for Gregorio's sake than my own. "Lord God of my father, please hear my prayer and save us from the sea. We don't deserve your mercy but we need it. We still want to become real boys, but I would be satisfied just with seeing Father again before I run down for good. As for Gregorio, please don't let him drown, even if You don't turn him into a boy again. You have been good to us before when we didn't deserve it. Now we're in the same boat again—or not in a boat, as the case is. Please save us and make us good; then we will be good."

I was still praying when Gregorio croaked out, "Pinocchio, an island!" My red-rimmed eyes snapped open and gazed over the dark lapping waves to where he was pointing with a limp antenna. I didn't need a hundred eyes to see it—a large black rock arched out of the water only a hundred yards in front of us. It was not an island, but might be called an islet; it was big enough to hold us at any rate. We could rest and recover our strength there and wait for a passing ship. Why, after drying out and soaking up some sun, Gregorio might even be able to fly on to the mainland.

"Lord, lead me to the rock that is higher than I," I exclaimed, parroting a line from the Bible. It seemed fitting, though I didn't really think about my words; I certainly wasn't giving sincere thanks to God for putting that wonderful rock right there where we needed it. I was to be far more sincere a mere minute later, when I would curse the very rock I was then in the act of blessing.

The current drew us swiftly towards the rock. A large cave yawned from the middle of its black face. The sea was running into the cave, disappearing into a deep crimson grotto. As we gaped in wonder the cave opened wide before our eyes. Palisades of polished white stones, looking for all the world like giant teeth, lined its mouth top and bottom. As the current swept us into the dark red cavern we realized, far too late to escape, that the stones were teeth indeed and that we had just been swallowed by a monstrous whale.

As the current swept us into the dark red cavern we realized, far too late to escape, that the stones were teeth indeed and that we had just been swallowed by a monstrous whale.

Chapter 34

The whale's massive jaws slammed shut. Hot, moist blackness wrapped around us like a shroud. I tried to scream, but panic gripped my throat and I could only gurgle a whimper. Gregorio's legs vibrated with fright, emitting a quavering squeal that soaked into the soft, fleshy walls about us and died without an echo.

Shock and horror dulled my brain. Shifting images of the fate awaiting me turned like a kaleidoscope in my head; I could not think one clear thought to save my life. Not that it mattered much—wit was not going to help us now. Time and again on our journey, I had deluded myself that brains and luck had gotten us out of one scrape after another. Each time, Gregorio had forced me to admit that it was the Lord who had delivered us, not my clever schemes; but after each danger was past, I returned to my vanity. Only now, that all my other thoughts were in disarray, did I see the truth clearly. And now it was too late; we had vanished from the face of the earth and from the presence of the Lord. What irony! It was no more than I deserved.

I came to myself again when I heard a soft, clear voice singing a hymn I knew:

> Sun of my soul, thou Savior dear,
> It is not night if thou be near.

Someone else was here, someone with a voice as sweet as an angel's, someone who believed the Lord was present even in this horrible black pit. My spirits revived a little and my brain began to work again.

Gregorio stopped shaking. "Is that you, Pinocchio? I always thought you couldn't carry a tune if your life depended on it."

"You're right about that; it's not me singing. Someone else is with us inside this beast. Hello! Hello!"

The sweet singer didn't answer my call. Gregorio lifted his head as if to look around, though even a hundred eyes could have seen nothing in there.

"Pinocchio, I've never known darkness like this, but the darkness is not all the same. When I turn towards the throat it seems, well, less dark in that direction—not that I see light or form or movement, but I sense a lesser darkness. Do you suppose there's a light of some sort deeper in? And the singer, she sounded far off; she can't be here in the mouth."

I looked and listened, but it seemed to me that inky silence lay about us equally in all directions. "Well, Gregorio, your eyes and ears are keener than mine, but I don't see or hear anything at all."

"All the same, I think we should paddle over to the throat and look into it to see what we can see."

"Absolutely not! If we stay in the mouth we may be able to make a dash for it the next time the whale opens his jaws, but if we venture into the depths of this monster we'll never escape."

We didn't have to argue out what our course would be, for just then the whale opened his mouth again and a wall of water washed us through the gullet and down into the belly. Like it or not, we were going further in, not back.

The incoming flood carried us into a high, ribbed vault that had to be the whale's belly. What a cesspool! Half-digested fish floated belly-up beside us in the stinking water; oily chocolate swirls coiled and uncoiled on its steaming surface. I could see as clearly as Gregorio now, for a bright light flared out over the water from the other end of the cavern. We splashed through the filth towards the light as fast as we could. What could it be?

As we approached the light we saw that it beamed cheerily from a lantern high on a pole planted in the middle of a large, well-made raft. I stopped at the edge of the raft and let my eyes range back and forth across the deck. There was no one on the raft.

"Come on, come on; the less time we spend in this fish's juices the better," gasped my friend behind me. "You'll have to help me," he continued, "I'm too weak to climb out of this slimy chowder." I hauled myself up on deck and pulled my friend after me. We lay there panting for a long time.

After a while I struggled to my feet. Clinging to the mast, I could stand and look around. Questions and fears crowded in on me.

"Gregorio, do you suppose this is Father's raft? It's so well-made that only a master craftsman like him could have built it. And the lantern looks a lot like one of ours, though I couldn't be sure of that. But if it's Father's raft, where is he?" I began to shout: "Father, Father!" The only sound that came back to me was the bubbling and gurgling of the rotting slop lapping at the raft. I bowed my head and began to cry softly.

Gregorio put a jointed arm around my shoulder. "I know what you're afraid of, Pinocchio, but use your wooden head to think, for once. The maker of the raft reached the bowels of the whale safely since the lantern is burning. But lanterns do not burn for long without being refilled. This lantern is still burning, so the maker of the raft has not been gone long. I'll bet your father is sculling around in a little dinghy somewhere farther in. He'll return to the raft shortly. I tell you…."

I cut my friend off: "Gregorio! Something's floating towards us, and it's not rotten fish. You've got a hundred eyes-can you make out what it is?" Gregorio peered into the dark waters. "It's a wooden box," he said. As he continued to watch the box approach all of my friend's eyes widened with astonishment. "Pinocchio, the box has our names on it!"

The box floated straight up to the raft. I grabbed it and swung it on deck. Sure enough, there were our names and another name as well:

TO: PINOCCHIO AND GREGORIO
FROM: GIOVANNI, SON OF GIUSEPPE

The box was nailed shut: how would I open it? I needed a tool. The lantern was fastened to the mast by a spike; that would do. I climbed up the mast and handed the lantern down to Gregorio. I worked the spike loose, shinnied down the mast, and began to pry the box open. Soon the lid was lying on the deck and we were able to look inside.

Lying inside the box on a bed of wood shavings were two corked bottles. One of the bottles contained a liquid, the other contained a scroll with writing. I uncorked the bottle with the scroll and began to read aloud:

> Dear Pinocchio and Gregorio,
>
> I imagine this message will reach you deep inside Leviatan, the great whale. He is hungry as the grave and has a way of finding shipwrecked mariners. Still, I trust the Lord to bring this message to you wherever you are.

> My father, Giuseppe, named me for Giovanni Battista, he who went before the Lord to prepare His way when He came to earth. I write this to prepare His way as He comes into your hearts.
>
> Pinocchio, after so many mishaps you know at last that you have no goodness in you to earn His favor, no way to cleanse yourself from the sin that stains you, and no way of escape from the whale, from death itself. You tried to be good; you failed again and again. You tried Doctor Moro's Method of Inner Change and his Method of Outer Change and you found that they didn't work. Now, at last, you know that you need the Lord. Now, at last, you are ready to hear the Lord's way of salvation. Now, at last, you are ready to hear my message, and receive it with faith.
>
> The message I have for you is a word of promise from the Lord Jesus, whose name is also Emmanuele. Do you know what the name Emmanuele means? It means, 'God with us.' That is exactly who Emmanuele is: God with us. You think you are alone, abandoned by God, but that is not true. He is in heaven now, but He is also with you there in the belly of the great whale. He is there to save you if you will only embrace Him in faith.
>
> Pinocchio, he will turn you into a real flesh-and-blood boy. The Bible says that God can turn stones into children of promise. If He can do that to stones He can certainly do it to a wooden boy. The Lord Jesus will wash the chocolate from you, Pinocchio, inside and out; He will wash away your sin and make you a child of God. And yes, He will rescue you from Leviatan, the great whale; He will rescue you from death, and bring you back to your father.

Gregorio burst out crying from a hundred eyes. "This is wonderful news for you, Pinocchio, but not for me. Wooden boys may be saved, but not crickets. I'm only an animal, and salvation is not for me. Giovanni's letter has no good news for me."

"Not so, Gregorio," I replied. "Giovanni has more to say in this letter, and the rest is directed to you." I continued reading:

> As for you, Gregorio, remember where you are. You are in the belly of a whale. Perhaps you do not know that one of God's prophets was also once in the belly of a whale. The prophet Giona did not want God to be merciful to his enemies; he wanted God to destroy their city. But the Lord told Giona that He would be merciful for the sake of the many people and cattle there. He made a point of mentioning the cattle, Gregorio! He cared even for the cattle, which were born animals and remained animals all their lives. He cares much more for you, who were born a real boy.
>
> But you, like Pinocchio, must repent of your sin and believe that the deliverance Jesus offers is intended for you, too. You are no more an insect in God's sight than Pinocchio or I; it is just that you have been given the grace to see the vileness of your sin and your need for salvation. What is required of you is faith in the Lord's promise to forgive you and make you a new creature.
>
> Your friend and servant for the sake of the Lord and Savior Jesus Christ.
>
> Giovanni

At those words, despair vanished from Gregorio's eyes—all of them—and he chirped for joy. My burden, too, was lifted. I doubted no more. The Lord Jesus was indeed God with us, Emmanuele, and He would do everything Giovanni had said.

Gregorio, who was reading over my shoulder, said, "It looks like there is a little more to Giovanni's letter, Pinocchio." Sure enough, at the bottom of the page was one more sentence:

> P.S. If you believe what I have written, open the other bottle and pour it into the water around the raft. Like the good news of Jesus Christ, the liquid within will be a fragrance of life for those who love Him but a fragrance of death to those who do not.

I uncorked the second bottle. Immediately the aroma of a flower garden in mid-summer overwhelmed our senses. The perfume was so sweet that I hesitated to pour it into the stinking slop lapping at the raft. But I knew, at long last, that a command from the Lord was to be obeyed. I emptied the bottle over the side.

Things happened fast. The water around us began to foam and froth, then to churn and slosh from one side of the monster's belly to the other. We clung tightly to the raft as it heaved up and down. Great Leviatan shuddered and shook wildly; then he belched. A blast of air, reeking of chocolate and corruption, propelled us up the gullet and out of his mouth.

We shot out into the bright sun and open sea. I turned and looked back in time to see Leviatan leap high in the air, spout water and steam, and plunge beneath the boiling foam. A great tidal wave washed out from the churning chaos where the monster sounded, overwhelming the raft, sweeping the deck clean, and washing us all into the sea. Then a wave dashed my head against a floating timber and I knew no more.

We shot out into the bright sun and open sea. I turned and looked back in time to see Leviatan leap high in the air, spout water and steam, and plunge beneath the boiling foam.

Chapter 35

Whether it was the pounding of my head, the pale sunshine falling on my face, or the cry of the gulls that woke me I don't know; I suppose it could have been the overpowering stench of rotting fish. I sat up to find myself on a mound of bunch grass just above the beach. The hazy morning sun was low in the sky, for it was almost winter, but the light breeze from the water was not cold. Oh, did my head ache! I touched my scalp gingerly and felt the swollen, tender flesh—the beam that struck me was no toothpick!

I must have fingered the lump on my head for a minute before the full truth sank in (you saw it right away, didn't you? The lump was real flesh!) I slapped my cheek and felt the blood rush to the skin; I gently bit my finger and saw the print of the teeth. I pulled a fine, auburn hair from my scalp and examined it in the morning light. I took off my shoes and watched my toes as I wiggled and folded them. My lips vibrated and my tongue trilled as I whistled like a bird in spring. I was a real boy!

I jumped to my feet and looked around for Gregorio. He was nowhere to be seen. Did I alone survive? A quarter mile down the beach I spied a round black rock jutting into the surf. I decided to climb it and get a better view of my surroundings. I began to trudge down the hard, damp sand towards the rock. As I drew near the rock I realized with a start that it was not a rock at all: it was a beached whale, none other than Leviatan himself!

I approached the looming hulk warily, puzzled, but not afraid. The monster couldn't see me, for his eyes had rolled back in his head and only the whites of his eyes showed. His rotting carcass fouled the salt air with the pungent smell that had wrinkled my new human nose hundreds of yards up the beach. Leviatan was as dead as a whale can be.

I dug down in my pocket and found my old handkerchief. Holding it over my nose to mask the putrid odor—a useless measure—I walked around to where I could look at my old terror head-on. My puzzlement grew: the beast's jaws were wide open, propped open by a wooden cross. I scratched my head—ouch!—and turned away. My eyes fell on a limp form stretched out on the sand just beyond the whale's open mouth—Gregorio! His insect armor lay split open and empty on the beach, already half-filled with sand from the ebb and flow of the tide.

I fell to my knees and sobbed uncontrollably, crying real tears for the first time. "Gregorio! We went through so much together! You were the one with the brains and the faith in the Lord; why was it I who lived and you who died? It would have been better for me to die too, or at least to remain wood; my pain would not be so great. I'm a real boy now—how I don't know—but I'll never be a happy one, grieving for you and Father."

"I can't let this go on anymore, Pinocchio, though it's nice to be appreciated. Turn away from that dead, stinking fish and come join the living."

I whirled around towards the voice I knew so well. Standing behind me with a big grin on his face and tears in his eyes was Gregorio, now a boy like me. Then my astonishment and joy grew greater as I saw Father standing behind my friend, beaming broadly.

"That's right, let me go on like a sentimental fool," I complained, but of course I couldn't be angry. I held my friend at arm's length and looked him up and down. "You look like the old Gregorio, all right, only a year older."

I turned to Father. We hugged each other wordlessly for a long time. Finally I spoke.

"I don't understand anything that's happened since we fled from the whale. How did Leviatan meet his end here on the beach? The last I saw of him he was diving deep into the sea, full of rage and spite. And the cross that holds open his mouth—How did that get there? Giovanni told us of the Lord Jesus and sent us a bottle of poison to make the whale vomit us out, but Giovanni couldn't make us real boys again, could he? Yet that is what we are, real boys at last. Even better, we are believers in Jesus Christ, God's Son. Whatever has happened?"

"Why don't you come and ask Giovanni all these questions yourself?" asked Father. "He's got a nice fire going on the other side of this sand dune, where he's fixing lunch for us."

I followed Father and Gregorio through clumps of dune grass up to the top of the ridge before us and down into a hollow between the dunes. A bed of coals smoldered in a fire pit in the bottom of

I whirled around towards the voice I knew so well. Standing behind me with a big grin on his face and tears in his eyes was Gregorio, now a boy like me. Then my astonishment and joy grew greater as I saw Father standing behind my friend, beaming broadly.

the hollow. There Giovanni squatted before the fire, broiling fish over the red-hot coals. I skidded down the sandy slope.

"We've been waiting for you to wake up, Pinocchio," said the clockmaker's son as I approached. "You must be hungry. Help yourself to the fish, but be careful, it's very hot. The firewood was well seasoned—do you recognize it?"

I knew at once that the glowing coals came from my old body, though I honestly couldn't spot any of my fingers or toes among the embers. One long glowing stick might have been my nose, but I wasn't sure. I did recognize the grill as the spring that had kept me going for nearly two years.

"Giovanni, I don't understand anything that has happened to us. Can you explain what you have done?"

"I did very little, Pinocchio. It is Jesus Christ, the Son of God, not Giovanni, the son of Giuseppe, who has done all this. He did just what He promised He would do. He cleansed you from your sin and made you His child through faith in Him. I simply delivered the message."

"But why did the whale vomit us out? Did the perfume kill him? And why is his mouth held open with a cross?"

"Patience, patience! I will explain all if you give me time. Leviatan was your grave. Our Savior delivered you from Leviatan and slew him to show you that the grave cannot hold those Christ makes alive. He makes us alive through faith in the gospel. The sweet perfume in the bottle was like the gospel of our Lord, a sweet fragrance of life to those who believe but a stench of death to those who are perishing.

"As for the cross holding Leviatan's mouth open, that was my idea. I found Leviatan dead on the beach. It came to me that forcing his mouth open with a cross would show all who pass by that it was through the cross that Christ conquered sin and death. Just then I spied your father walking towards me on the beach. He was swept off his raft the night of the big storm and was washed ashore right here. The whale got the raft, but the Lord delivered your father.

"I told your father my idea. He knows how to work with wood so he made the cross. Together we succeeded in propping Leviatan's mouth open and jamming the cross between his jaws. While we were doing all this you were sleeping peacefully up the beach, where the tide washed you in."

"You have only begun to answer my questions," I said. "What about Gregorio's body? It's lying back there on the beach."

"As for the empty body that brought tears to your eyes, it's the husk the Lord Christ cast aside when He made Gregorio a real boy again. Don't ever think it was just another molt. You watched your friend molt ten times on Doctor Moro's island, and each time he emerged a cricket again. When the Lord changes you He makes you a new creature entirely. "

"I have another question."

"Ask, by all means."

"If Father was washed off his raft in the big storm, he has been here for over a week. But the lantern on the raft was still burning. How could that be?"

"I don't know, but surely it was the Lord's doing."

"I have one more question: When we were surrounded by darkness in the whale's mouth, I was overcome with despair until I heard a sweet voice, like an angel's it seemed. Is the singer here? Did she escape the whale? Was it the voice of Gabriela I heard?"

"I'm sure it was not your imagination. Like the burning lantern, I believe the Lord sent the singer to give you faith and hope in your darkest hour."

"Then it was the voice of the angel Gabriele, not the girl Gabriela!" exclaimed Gregorio.

"You two will have to keep on wondering till you get home and ask Gabriela herself," laughed Giovanni. "Meanwhile, after we've eaten, I'm going to reforge that old spring into something more useful for you and Gregorio. We leave tomorrow for home."

I had more questions for Giovanni and we talked all day, till the watery winter sun sank into a cloudbank hanging over the water. Dusk fell, but the sandy hollow remained warm. We all grew sleepy except Giovanni. He bade us goodnight, then walked down to the beach to pray.

When we awoke in the morning, a chilly fog had settled down in the hollow. We went down to the beach and dragged back a great quantity of driftwood, which we were able to ignite with a handful of coals that had burned through the night.

After breakfast, it was time to start on the long road home.

"After you went to bed, I forged these for our journey," said Giovanni, handing Gregorio and me two short, unadorned swords.

"I made them from your mainspring, Pinocchio. Such fine Milano steel ought not to end up as a grill! We may need them on the way home, and you and Gregorio will certainly need them later if you are serious about following the Lord Christ, for He has many enemies still."

"But Giovanni, I know so little about the Lord! A sword will do me no good at all. How will I know who His enemies are? I have been fooled so many times! How will I know His will? I have followed my own way and thought it was pleasing to God so many times! I need a Bible, not a sword!"

"Well said, Pinocchio! The Bible is the sword of the Spirit; it is what you really need if you are to be a follower of Christ. We cannot make a Bible out of Milano steel; you will have to wait till we can find a Bible for you. Still, swords sometimes prove useful."

We strapped on the swords and began trudging across the dunes towards the coastal road.

Chapter 36

Father set the cake on the table in front of us. This time the cake was a white cake with creamy yellow frosting, not a chocolate cake such as had been my undoing. The cake was even bigger than the cake that caused all the trouble in the first place. No, I can't blame the cake; the guilt was mine alone. But that seemed like a long time ago now that I was sitting with friends and family around the table for my much delayed birthday party. Father had invited just a few close friends: Giuseppe, Giovanni, Gregorio, and Gabriela.

"We are here to celebrate your birthday with you, Pinocchio," said Giovanni, who by common consent served as master of ceremonies. "Let us give thanks for this happy occasion:

"Lord God, we thank you that you have brought Pinocchio to this day. He celebrates this birthday as a real boy, not as a manikin that needs to be wound up with a spring. Better, he celebrates this birthday as a boy who has been saved from his sin and is a child of yours. His salvation is your work, Lord, and we thank you for it. Continue your work in him, Lord. Make him to know your will and your ways better each passing day. Grant him to grow in the grace and knowledge of Christ. Now bless this food to all our bodies. In the Savior's Name we pray, Amen."

Father cut generous pieces of cake for us all. After we had eaten, it was time for gifts.

Giuseppe gave me a new suit of clothes. After all I had been through, the fine green and yellow outfit I wore when I started out on my quest was ragged, stained, shrunken by sea water, and quite disreputable. Giuseppe was fond of red and blue, so my new outfit was quite a change. But I had begun a new life and was ready to adopt a new fashion to go with it. Father assured me that he liked red and blue almost as much as he liked green and yellow. I went in the back room, changed my clothes, and returned to the party, where my new look received the enthusiastic approval of everyone.

Giovanni announced that he had already given me my birthday gift.

"I had to give Pinocchio his gift early. The swords that I made for him and Gregorio are my gift. I feared they might need them on the trip home, though by God's mercy they did not. But if Pinocchio is serious about serving the Lord Christ in this world, he may be glad for his sword."

Gregorio spoke next: "Pinocchio is my dearest friend in the world. We've gone through so much together that no one except the Lord knows. My gift for you, Pinocchio, is a diary. I want you to write down everything that's happened to you. No, that's not right. I want you to write down all the Lord has done in your life. Your life has been in His hands from the time Gepetto carved your lifeless wooden parts up until now. Someday someone may read your diary and give God the glory for all He has done for you. As for you, as you read it over you will be reminded of how He delivered you in spite of your own efforts, which only made things worse. In that way you may be preserved from pride and further foolishness and harm."

"Thank you, I think," I said, taking the diary. (I hope, dear reader, that you know you are reading that diary at this moment.)

It was Gabriela's turn. With a shy smile she handed me a small package wrapped in tissue paper. I unfolded the tissue slowly, trying to hide my eagerness to see what the girl I loved had for me. Turning back the last sheet of tissue, I discovered a locket on a chain. Opening the locket, I found a lock of gleaming jet-black hair, more shiny than the locket itself.

"I know the Lord will take you far away in His service before you finally return home to stay, Pinocchio. Please wear this locket as a reminder of me. I will wait for you, Pinocchio, and I will pray for you. Let the locket be your assurance of that." Embarrased at her own words, Gabriela said no more. I was at a loss for words, too.

Father gave me his gift last. It was a Bible.

"Giovanni told me what you said to him when he gave you the swords. For the first time in your life you admitted that you needed wisdom and knowledge from God. You will find that in this book, Pinocchio. Read it, study it. It is teaching, reproof, correction, and instruction in righteousness. By mastering it you will be fully equipped for any work God has for you."

Then Father brought out another package and handed it to Gregorio. My friend eagerly removed the colorful paper to find that he, too, had a Bible now.

Father gave me his gift last. It was a Bible.
"Giovanni told me what you said to him when he gave you the swords. For the first time in your life you admitted that you needed wisdom and knowledge from God. You will find that in this book, Pinocchio…."

"Just because it's not your birthday doesn't mean that you should go home tonight with a full stomach and empty hands, Gregorio. I suspect that you and Pinocchio will leave this little village together in the service of the Savior. You, too, need to know God's Word if you are to live for Him and serve Him."

I thanked everyone as well as I could, being a little choked up. Then we all ate another piece of cake. Our guests departed after wishing me a happy birthday one more time.

"Time for bed, Pinocchio," said Father when they all had gone. We each went to our rooms, but I wasn't sleepy. After lying there a short while, I sat up in bed. I lit my candle, opened my Bible and began to read. I had so much to learn if I was to live for Him Who had changed me from a wooden boy soaked in sin into a child of God.

PINOCCHIO'S HOME
ROMAGNANO
VERCELLI
CASALE
PO RIVER
TORINO
ALESSANDRIA
NOVI
GENOA
PORTOFINO
DR. MORO'S ISLAND
LIGURIAN SEA
ITALY
ADRIATIC SEA
CORSICA
SARDINIA
TYRRHENIAN SEA
SICILY